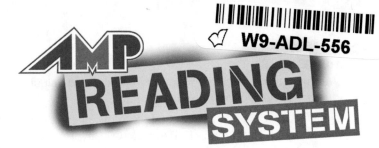

AMP READING SYSTEM

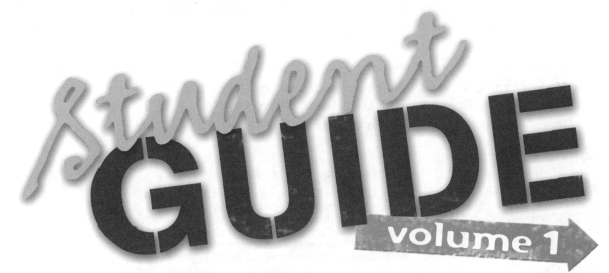

Student GUIDE
volume 1

PROGRAM AUTHOR
Timothy Shanahan, Ph.D.
Professor of Urban Education at the University of Illinois at Chicago
Director of the UIC Center for Literacy.

GLOBE FEARON
Pearson Learning Group

REVIEWERS

We thank the following educators who provided valuable comments and suggestions during the development of the Student Guides:

Debi Glanton, Conyers, GA; Karen S. McDaniels, Miami, FL; Irene G. Mortensen, Quakertown, NJ; Yvonne E. Paranick, Oil City, PA; Sr. Mary Jean Raymond, Cleveland, OH; Maria Schneider, Ft. Myers, FL; Vickie L. Scraper, Wichita, KS; Dr. Margaret M. Smith, Las Vegas, NV

PROJECT STAFF

Art and Design: Tricia Battipede, Evelyn Bauer, Sharon Bozek, Bernadette Hruby, Salita Mehta, Elizabeth Nemeth, Alison O'Brien, April Okano, Angel Weyant

Editorial: Laura Axler, Leslie Feierstone Barna, Brian Hawkes, Cindy Kane, Madeline Boskey Olsen, Patricia Peters, Jennie Rakos, Emily Shenk, Constance Shrier, Maury Solomon, Tara Walters, Shirley White

Inventory: Jean Wohlgemuth

Marketing: Ken Clinton, Andrea Spaeth

Production/Manufacturing: Irene Belinsky, Laura Benford-Sullivan, Carlos Blas, Mark Cirillo, Jeff Engel, Leslie Greenberg, Ruth Leine, Susan Levine, Karyn Mueller

Publishing Operations: Richetta Lobban, Kate Matracia, Debi Schlott

PHOTO AND ILLUSTRATION CREDITS

All photography © Pearson Education, Inc. (PEI) unless otherwise specifically noted.

Cover: *t.l.* Eric Meola/Image Bank/Getty Images, Inc.; *r.* The Image Bank/Getty Images, Inc.; *b.l.* © David Stoecklien/Corbis. 1: *t.l.* © David Stoecklien/Corbis; *r.* Jack Hollingsworth/Photodisc/Getty Images, Inc. 6: AP/Wide World Photo. 12: Nathan Bilow/Allsport/Getty Images, Inc. 18: Index Stock Imagery/ PictureQuest. 24: © Kevin Fleming/Corbis. 33: AP/Wide World Photo. 39: Philip Gatward/DK Images. 42: 94-339, UM79-1, 7(VII)35, K. Ross Toole Archive, The University of Montana—Missoula/Mike and Maureen Mansfield Library, University of Montana, Missoula. 48: Photo by © Shelly Castellano/Zuma Press. 54: AP/Wide World Photo. 56: *t.r.* National Geographic/Getty Images, Inc.; *b.r.* PhotoDisc, Inc.; *t.l.* The Image Bank/Getty Images, Inc.; *r.* Jack Hollingsworth/Photodisc/Getty Images, Inc. 62: David R. Frazier Photography. 68: Alistair Duncan/DK Images. 74: The Art Archive/Egyptian Museum Turin/Dagle Orti/The Picture Desk/The Art Archive/Kobal. 80: The Art Archive/National Anthropological Museum Mexico/Dagli Orti/The Picture Desk/The Art Archive/ Kobal. 83: The Art Archive/Musée du Louvre Paris/Dagli Orti/The Picture Desk /The Art Archive/Kobal. 89: © Bettmann/Corbis. 98: The Image Bank/Getty Images, Inc. 109: © Reuters/Corbis. 110: Dean Rutz/ *The Seattle Times.* 112: *t.r.* © Reuters/Corbis; *b.r.* PhotoDisc, Inc.; *t.l.* Eric Meola/Image Bank/Getty Images, Inc.; *r.* Jack Hollingsworth/Photodisc/Getty Images, Inc. 118: © Jonathan Blair/Corbis. 124: Danny Johnston/ AP/Wide World Photo. 130 Dave King/DK Images. 139: Boltin Picture Library. 145: © Keren Su/Corbis. 151: AP/Wide World Photo. 154: Eyewire Collection/Getty Images, Inc. 160: Pal Hermansen/Stone/Getty Images, Inc. 168: *t.l.* Steven Nourse/Stone/Getty Images, Inc.; *b.r.* PhotoDisc, Inc.

Illustrations: All coach characters on vocabulary "Your Turn" pages: KATMO. 5: Kagan McLeod. 27: Tom Frost. 32: Nicole Ray. 61: Maria Raymondsdotter. 67: Shane Evans. 82: Monika Melnychuk. 95, 97: Kagan McLeod. 104: James Elston. 117: Sheila Aldridge. 135: Dan Trush. 136: Monika Melnychuk. 165: James Elston. 166: Paul Mirocha.

ISBN: 0-13-024725-1

Printed in the United States of America

4 5 6 7 8 9 10 08 07 06

Globe Fearon
Pearson Learning Group

1-800-321-3106
www.pearsonlearning.com

CONTENTS

Fluency
Use periods to tell when to pause, 6, 12. Read phrases instead of individual words, 18. Read difficult sentences smoothly, 24. Scan for unfamiliar words and find out their meaning, 27. Read with expression, 33. Vary volume and expression to make reading more interesting, 39, 42. Read at a comfortable pace, 48. Read in a smooth, relaxed manner, as in conversation, 54.

UNIT 2 *Colossal Constructions continued*

Read on Your Own 60, 63, 66, 69, 72, 75, 78, 81, 84, 87, 90, 93, 96, 99, 102, 105, 108, 111

Fluency

Find out how to pronounce difficult words before reading, 62. Read with natural expression, 68. Read every word, 74. Read dialogue with expression, 80. Match expression to content, 83, 95. Use punctuation marks as clues to expression and phrasing, 89, 98. Read smoothly and at a natural pace, 104. Identify difficult sentences before reading, 110.

UNIT 3

Great Unsolved Mysteries

Read on Your Own 116, 119, 122, 125, 128, 131, 134, 137, 140, 143, 146, 149, 152, 155, 158, 161, 164, 167

Fluency

Use punctuation marks as clues to expression and phrasing, 118. Practice difficult words and sentences before reading, 124, 130, 139. Read dialogue with expression, 136, 160. Read smoothly and match pace to content, 145, 166. Match expression to content, 151, 154.

Sports on the Edge

Edge

COMPREHENSION
LEARN THE STEPS TO A GOOD SUMMARY

INDEPENDENT READING
Sports on the Edge
Includes "Extreme Sports" and
"Unusual Moments in Sports"

unit 1

VOCABULARY

WORDS:
Know them!
Use them!
Learn all about them!

FLUENCY
Make your reading
smooth and accurate,
one tip at a time

Make Words Yours!

Learn the WORDS

Here are some words you will be reading in the next weeks. They are also words you need to know for your everyday reading.

WORD AND EXPLANATION	EXAMPLE	WRITE AN EXAMPLE
If something is **challenging**, it takes hard work or skill. **Challenging** is the opposite of *easy*.	Running may be easy, but running a marathon is **challenging**.	What's the most **challenging** thing you've done this week?
Expert describes someone with a lot of knowledge or skill in something. Someone who is an **expert** has special knowledge or skill.	Someone might be an **expert** speller. A scientist who knows a lot about bugs is an **expert**.	What is another kind of **expert**?
A **feature** is an important part of something.	Bleachers are one **feature** of a gym.	What **features** does your classroom have?
Something that is **immense** is very large or huge.	On my first day, the new school seemed **immense**.	What animals are **immense**?
When you do something **mental**, you use your mind, such as thinking and solving problems.	Adding a list of numbers in your head is a **mental** activity.	What is another **mental** activity?
Merely means only.	Of course she can't understand it; she's **merely** a child.	What interesting places are **merely** a few hours away?
When you do something **physical**, you use your body.	Riding a bicycle or lifting weights helps build **physical** strength.	What else can you do to build **physical** strength?
If something is **required**, you must have or must do it.	Drivers are **required** to use safety belts.	What activities have you done today that were **required**?

YOUR TURN

Answer these questions and be ready to explain your answers.

1. Is singing less *challenging* than playing an instrument? _____

2. If you have *merely* scratched your arm, is it serious? _____

3. If a project seems *immense*, will you need help to do it? _____

4. Is swimming a *mental* exercise? _____

Choose the right word

challenging   required   merely   mental
feature   immense   physical   expert

Fill each blank with the correct word from the box.

5. A lot of sports are mental and not just _____.

6. Keisha felt _____ happiness when she won the award.

7. A large lake is the main _____ of our park.

8. Should a helmet be _____ when you ride a bike?

9. Tami is an _____ at knitting.

10. Memorizing the multiplication table takes good _____ powers.

11. It is _____ a shower; the rain will stop soon.

12. Jamal only plays sports that he finds _____.

Now show that you know the words by writing some things you already know about challenging sports.

Show that you know

Complete the sentences.

13. For dangerous sports, players should be *required* to _____

14. One *feature* of paintball probably is _____

15. A helmet can keep a player from *physical* injury because _____

16. To become an *expert* you should _____

READ on your OWN
Sports on the Edge, pages 3–6

BEFORE YOU READ

Think about what you already know about extreme sports. Why do you think people like to play them?

AS YOU READ

Read "Extremely Extreme," pages 3–5. (STOP)
Complete the sentence below to tell what the chapter is about.

Athletes compete in extreme sports in the _____

_____

Read page 6 of "Skateboards in the Sky." (STOP)
Complete the sentence below to tell what the page is about.

Bored surfers put wheels on surfboards to _____

_____

_____

VOCABULARY
Watch for the words you are learning about.

feature: display

immensely: greatly

experts: people with special skill or knowledge

mere: simple

FLUENCY
Pay attention to punctuation marks as you read.

AFTER YOU READ

Which extreme sport have you heard about, in these pages or elsewhere, that you might like to try? Why?

↓ SUMMARIZE: Topic

How to Summarize

Step 1
Identify the **topic**. Ask, *Who or what is this about?*

Step 2
Identify the **main idea**. Ask, *What is the main thing the writer is saying about the topic?*

Step 3
Identify the **important details**. Ask, *What details are needed to understand the main idea?*

Step 4
Use the main idea and important details to **summarize**.

Learn the STRATEGY

When you summarize, you briefly retell something in your own words. You identify the most important things in the section you are reading. Good readers summarize because it helps them remember what they read.

To begin summarizing, look for the topic. The **topic** is a word or phrase that answers the question, *Who or what is this about?*

When you summarize, you want to tell only the most important ideas. Good summaries do not include a lot of extra facts. In the cartoon below, what is Troy talking about? What is Angie thinking?

What is the **topic** of Troy's sentences?

a. a football game
b. how to play football
c. choosing teams
d. his friends

What is the **topic** of Angie's thoughts?

a. her favorite sport
b. summarizing
c. a football game
d. her friends

Hey, Angie, guess what? In the first quarter, the Hawks scored a field goal. Then, the Eagles scored a touchdown to make the score 7–3. In the second quarter, the Eagles kicked a field goal to add to their lead. The Hawks scored a touchdown right before halftime to make the score 10–10. Neither team scored in the third quarter, so the game was tied. Then, they . . .

Oh, boy. This could go on forever. It will take days to find out who won. Couldn't Troy just summarize?

➤ YOUR TURN

Read "Splat!" Then answer the numbered questions.

Splat!

1. The sentences in this paragraph tell about a single topic. What is it?

A bright red ball of paint flies by and hits the tree behind me. That was close! I'm playing paintball, and it's a **challenging** game. What is paintball? It's like playing tag at the same time you're playing hide and seek. The main **feature** of paintball is the colorful balls of paint that players shoot at one another. The game is played in two teams. When players are hit, they are **required** to leave the game. Each team guards a flag—and each team tries to get the other team's flag.

2. What is the topic of this paragraph?

More than half of my team has been hit and I decide that it's time for some strategy. I look around the **immense** playing field and see that three players from the other team are guarding their flag, so I duck behind a tree while one of my teammates sneaks up on the guards. Then I lean out, take aim, and shoot. Splat! I hit one of the guards with a yellow paintball. "Right on, Adam!" my teammate yells. We have a chance of winning now! I aim again to zap one of the other guards. Splat! I'm out.

3. Look at the topic of each paragraph. What is the topic of "Splat!"?

Scan the passage and circle the periods. As you reread, use the circles to tell you when to pause.

FLUENCY

READ on your OWN
Sports on the Edge, pages 7–9

BEFORE YOU READ

Think about the last pages you read in "Extreme Sports." Why were skateboards invented?

AS YOU READ

Read "Getting Vertical," pages 7–8. (STOP)
Write the topic below.

Topic: _____

_____

Read "Hitting the Competitions," page 9. (STOP)
Write the topic below.

Topic: _____

_____

VOCABULARY
Watch for the words you are learning about.

challenging: difficult

required: needed

featured: gave importance to

FLUENCY
Use periods, question marks, and exclamation points to tell you when to pause.

AFTER YOU READ

Choose the most interesting section or page. What one new fact have you learned?

Get Wordwise!
The Suffix -ly

Learn More About the WORDS

Below are some words you have studied. Often you will see these words with **-ly** added. Adding **-ly** to a word slightly changes the meaning of the word.

The **-ly** ending is called a **suffix**. A suffix is a word part added to the end of a word to change its meaning slightly. Adding the suffix **-ly** to a word tells *how* something is done.

WORD	EXPLANATION	ADD -ly TO THE WORD	WRITE AN EXAMPLE
expert	Someone who is **expert** at a job does it really well.	Because she had practiced, she played _____.	What can you do **expertly**?
immense	If something is **immense**, it is really big. Just saying it's large wouldn't be enough.	I'll be _____ sad if you move away.	What is something **immensely** interesting?
mere	To call something **mere** is to make it seem unimportant.	I'm not really sick; it's _____ a cold.	How would you feel if the star athlete's performance was **merely** average?
physical	When you do something **physical**, you use your body.	After playing soccer in gym class, I feel really good _____.	Do you feel best **physically** in the morning or at night?
mental	When you do something **mental**, you use your mind.	I didn't feel as though I was _____ ready for the big game.	What is the best time of day for you **mentally**?

→YOUR TURN

Choose the right word

expertly   merely   mentally   physically   immensely

Fill in the blanks with the best *-ly* word from the box. Use each word once.

1. The workout in gym class made me _____ fit.

2. The teacher was _____ pleased with Jen's work.

3. Be patient! I _____ asked you to wait a minute.

4. The skateboarder made all his moves _____ .

5. The spelling contest was _____ challenging.

> Show that you know about the suffix *-ly* by answering questions about sports.

Which word works?

Circle the correct word in each pair.

6. The doctor was **expert** / **expertly** at stitching cuts closed.

7. I've seen it done less **expert** / **expertly**.

8. Getting all the students to agree was an **immense** / **immensely** challenge.

9. The program features activities that are **immense** / **immensely** popular.

10. It was **mere** / **merely** a little scratch.

11. She was a **mere** / **merely** child, and the dog frightened her.

12. Training helps to build **physical** / **physically** strength.

13. After the race, he was **physical** / **physically** exhausted.

14. Are you **mental** / **mentally** prepared for this test?

15. This puzzle is a **mental** / **mentally** nightmare!

Show that you know

Answer each question. Use sentences.

16. Which sport do you think is most *physically* challenging?

17. Which sport do you think is most *mentally* challenging?

18. Which indoor sports are *immensely* popular?

Unit 1, Lesson 3   9

READ on your OWN
Sports on the Edge, pages 10–12

BEFORE YOU READ

Think about the last pages you read in "Extreme Sports." What are some tricks that skateboarders do?

AS YOU READ

Read pages 10–11 of "Snowboarders Hit the Big Time." (STOP)
Write the topic below.

Topic: _____

_____

Read "From Snurfer to Snowboard," pages 11–12. (STOP)
Write the topic below.

Topic: _____

_____

VOCABULARY

Watch for the words you are learning about.

merely: only

challenges: things that call for hard work

expert: having a lot of knowledge or skill in something

immense: very large

FLUENCY

Remember to use periods, question marks, and exclamation points as clues to tell you when to pause.

AFTER YOU READ

Which style of snowboarding did you find most interesting? Why?

SUMMARIZE: Main Idea

How to Summarize

Step 1	Step 2	Step 3	Step 4
Identify the **topic**. Ask, *Who or what is this about?*	Identify the **main idea**. Ask, *What is the main thing the writer is saying about the topic?*	Identify the **important details**. Ask, *What details are needed to understand the main idea?*	Use the main idea and important details to **summarize**.

Learn the STRATEGY

You have practiced Step 1, identifying the topic. Now look at Step 2, identifying the main idea. Knowing the topic can help you figure out the main idea. The **main idea** is what the writer wants to tell you about the topic. Any summary should include the author's main idea.

Often, you can find the main idea stated in a sentence. Sometimes it is in the first or second sentence. Sometimes it is in the last sentence. Find the main-idea sentence in the first paragraph of the passage below.

Sometimes the main idea isn't stated, and you have to figure it out. That's what you'll do for the second paragraph.

What sport lets you soar through the air as free as a bird? It's bungee jumping. Bungee jumping has become a very popular sport. During the past 25 years, millions of people have successfully jumped. Bungee-jumping companies are thriving. Bungee-jumping clubs have sprung up all over the world.

A bungee jumper wears a harness that is attached to a cord made of elastic or rubber. The other end of the cord is connected to a high place such as a bridge. First, the jumper dives from the high place. The cord stretches as far as it can until the jumper is close to the ground or the water. Then, the cord springs back and the jumper flies upward.

What is the **main-idea** sentence of the first paragraph?

a. There are bungee jumping clubs all over the world.
b. Bungee jumping has become a very popular sport.
c. You will soar through the air like a bird.

What is the unstated **main idea** of the second paragraph?

a. Bungee jumping is jumping from a high place and springing back.
b. A bungee jumper wears a harness that is attached to a cord.
c. One end of the cord is connected to a high place such as a bridge.

➤YOUR TURN

Read "Bungee Jumping." Then follow the numbered directions.

Bungee Jumping

1. Write the topic.

2. Complete the main idea.
Bungee jumping started

3. Write the topic.

4. Complete the main idea.
Bungee cords

Bungee jumping is based on a tradition that comes from an island in the South Pacific. Boys tie one end of a vine around their ankles and fasten the other end to the top of a tower. Then they jump. This act shows both their **physical** and their **mental** courage. It proves that they are now men.

In the 1970s, members of a sports club heard about the tradition. They decided to try it. Their cord was **merely** a braided rubber rope tied around their ankles. Ten years later, A. J. Hackett saw a video of these jumpers. He decided to find a safe way to jump. He tested different cords with different bridge heights and people of different weights. Finally, he developed a new, safer bungee cord. The new, safer cords helped Hackett and many others like him become **expert** bungee jumpers.

5. Now choose the main idea of "Bungee Jumping."
   a. Boys in the South Pacific use vines instead of cords when they jump from the top of a tower.
   b. Bungee jumping started as a tradition using vines and is now a sport that uses safer cords.
   c. The first bungee cords were braided rubber ropes.
   d. Hackett made a safer cord and became an expert jumper.

Scan the passage and circle the commas. As you reread, use the circles to tell you when to pause briefly.

FLUENCY

READ on your OWN
Sports on the Edge, pages 13–15

BEFORE YOU READ

Think about the last pages you read in "Extreme Sports." How are snowboarders like skiers? How are they like surfers? How are they like skateboarders?

AS YOU READ

Read "Snowboards Rule!" page 13. (STOP)
Fill in that part of the chart below.

Read "Meet Shaun White," page 14. (STOP)
Fill in that part of the chart.

Read "What's Next?" page 15. (STOP)
Fill in that part of the chart.

VOCABULARY
Watch for the words you are learning about.

featured: gave importance to

mere: only

required: made to

physical: relating to the body, not the mind

mental: relating to the mind, not the body

FLUENCY
Remember to use commas as clues to tell you when to pause.

Snowboards Rule!	*Meet Shaun White*	*What's Next?*
Topic	Topic	Topic
Main Idea *One change in snowboarding was*	**Main idea** *Shaun White is one of the*	**Main idea** *Two new things in snowboarding are*

AFTER YOU READ

Do you think snowboarding should be an Olympic sport? Why or why not?

Make Words Yours!

Learn the WORDS

As you read more about extreme sports, you'll come across these words. This is your chance to get to know them better.

WORD AND EXPLANATION	EXAMPLE	WRITE AN EXAMPLE
The **location** of something is the place where it is.	Nobody knew the **location** of the party.	What is your favorite **location** for watching television?
Something **majestic** is impressive and grand.	From the bridge, we saw the **majestic** Statue of Liberty.	What is something else you would describe as **majestic**?
A **method** is a way or plan for doing something.	One **method** of cooking eggs is frying them.	What is a **method** of transportation?
If something is **normal**, it is regular, average, or usual.	On a **normal** morning, you probably wake up, get dressed, and go to school.	What is part of your **normal** day?
An **outcome** of something is how it turns out.	We were eager to learn the **outcome** of the race.	What is an **outcome** you are eager to know about?
To **range** is to be within certain limits, such as questions that **range** from easy to challenging.	The age of students in the class **ranged** from five to nine.	What is something else that **ranges** from easy to challenging?
A **route** is the way you take to get somewhere.	I can take two different **routes** to school.	What is the **route** you take to your best friend's home?
Something that is an **undertaking** is a project, usually a large one.	Cleaning up the empty lot was a big **undertaking** for the class.	What is a big **undertaking** you have been part of?

►YOUR TURN

Answer these questions and be ready to explain your answers.

1. Is the best *route* always the shortest one? _____

2. Would something *majestic* get your attention? _____

3. Do you enjoy movies *ranging* from comedies to action films? _____

4. If you have a *method* for doing something, have you done it before? _____

Choose the right word

location	majestic	method	normal
outcome	range	route	undertaking

Fill each blank with the correct word from the box.

5. Mia took a different _____ to school every day.

6. It's not _____ for a team to win every single game.

7. Being the head coach of the soccer team is a huge _____.

8. Her crown made the queen look _____.

9. We didn't learn the _____ of the election until midnight.

10. His interests _____ from reading to hiking.

11. The exact _____ of the treasure was unknown.

12. Kyle learned a new _____ of working out.

Now that you know about bungee jumping, show that you know the words by making some guesses about the sport.

Show that you know

Complete the sentences.

13. If you were bungee jumping, it would be *normal* to feel

14. An *undertaking* like learning to bungee jump would be

15. The perfect *outcome* of bungee jumping would be

16. The best *location* for bungee jumping is

READ on your OWN
Sports on the Edge, pages 16–19

BEFORE YOU READ

Think about the last pages you read in "Extreme Sports." Who is Shaun White?

AS YOU READ

Read pages 16–17 of "BMX Beasts." (STOP)
Fill in that part of the chart below.

Read "Freestyle Flavors," pages 18–19. (STOP)
Fill in that part of the chart.

VOCABULARY
Watch for the words you are learning about.

route: the way you take to get somewhere

normal: regular or average

range: how much something can change

method: a way of doing something

majestic: very impressive

undertaking: task

FLUENCY
Remember that commas are used to tell a reader when to pause briefly.

BMX Beasts	*Freestyle Flavors*
Topic	**Topic**
Main idea *BMX started when bike riders raced their bikes on motocross tracks and began*	**Main idea** *Today, there are special BMX bikes, riders are better, and*

AFTER YOU READ

Which BMX bike stunts seem like the most fun to do or watch? Explain your answer.

SUMMARIZE: Important Details

How to Summarize

Step 1	Step 2	Step 3	Step 4
Identify the **topic**. Ask, *Who or what is this about?*	Identify the **main idea**. Ask, *What is the main thing the writer is saying about the topic?*	Identify the **important details**. Ask, *What details are needed to understand the main idea?*	Use the main idea and important details to **summarize**.

Learn the STRATEGY

You have practiced Steps 1 and 2, identifying the topic and the main idea. Now look for **important details** that help you understand the main idea. Details are small points that explain something or add information about something.

When you look for important details, ask yourself, *Does this detail help me understand the main idea? Is it important?* If a detail doesn't help you figure out the main idea, it is not important. Focusing on only the important details will help you understand and remember what you have read.

To learn how to hang glide, you don't just jump off a cliff. You need to take a course at a hang-gliding school. First, you learn how to take off and land. These are the hardest parts of hang gliding and also the most important. Next, you learn to fly low skims above the ground. As you get better, you'll learn to fly higher and to make gentle turns. At this point, you're really enjoying yourself. When you complete the course, you have to pass a test before you can make a solo flight.

What is the **topic** of the paragraph?

a. how to take off and land
b. learning to hang glide
c. making a solo flight

The **main idea** is that you learn to hang glide by taking a course. Which three **details** are most important?

a. You don't just jump off a cliff.
b. You learn how to take off and land.
c. You enjoy yourself at this point.
d. You have to pass a test.
e. You make a solo flight.

➤ YOUR TURN

Read "Hang Gliding." Then follow the numbered directions.

HANG GLIDING

1. Underline the most important details—the ones that help you understand this main idea:
I got ready to hang glide.

2. Underline the most important details—the ones that help you understand this main idea:
I let the wind take me on an adventure.

3. Underline the most important details—the ones that help you understand this main idea:
My first solo flight was a success!

"Ready for takeoff," I said anxiously as I stood on the edge of a mountain. It is not **normal** for me to get nervous before a hang-gliding flight, but this time, I was hang gliding alone, and it felt like a big **undertaking**. I checked my harness and helmet—they were on tight. I firmly gripped the control bar. The wind was blowing in the right direction, so I started running down the steep, grassy slope.

Suddenly, I was flying. I purposely hadn't planned a **route**. I just let the wind take me on an incredible adventure. When I looked down, I saw a hawk flying above the forest below. I shifted my weight so I could turn and follow the hawk. The next thing I knew, I could see nothing but clouds. When I got through them, I saw **majestic** mountaintops covered with snow.

For the next hour I flew, twisting and turning, dipping up and down. I couldn't believe I was hang gliding! When it was time to land, I pushed the control bar as far out as I could. The glider slowed down, and I made a smooth landing. My first solo flight was a success!

Reread the passage and try to make your reading smoother. Practice reading phrases, or groups of words, instead of individual words.

FLUENCY

READ on your OWN
Sports on the Edge, pages 20–22

BEFORE YOU READ

Think about the last pages you read in "Extreme Sports." How many kinds of moves are there in BMX freestyle?

AS YOU READ

Read "The Ups and Downs of Learning," pages 20–21. (STOP)
Fill in that part of the chart below.

Read "BMX Experts," pages 21–22. (STOP)
Fill in that part of the chart.

VOCABULARY
Watch for the words you are learning about.

normal: regular or average

undertaking: big project

majestic: grand

FLUENCY
Reread sentences that you have trouble with. Rereading should help you read more smoothly.

The Ups and Downs of Learning	BMX Experts
Main idea	**Main idea**
Important details	**Important details**

AFTER YOU READ

What is the most interesting thing you learned about BMX biking?

Get Wordwise!
Synonyms and Antonyms

Learn More About the WORDS

Some words mean about the same thing as other words. For example, *big* and *large* mean about the same thing. Words that have similar meanings are called **synonyms**.

Some words have opposite, or very different, meanings. For example, *big* and *little* have opposite meanings. Words that have opposite meanings are called **antonyms**.

WORD	EXAMPLE SENTENCE	SYNONYM OR ANTONYM?
challenging	Studying for an exam can be extremely **challenging**.	Doug thought that it would be **easy** to learn how to play the guitar. _____
immense	There is an **immense** number of fish in the ocean.	Jenny's game-winning shot was **huge**. _____
majestic	The view from the top of the mountain was **majestic**.	When Karyn visited the old castle, she thought it was very **impressive**. _____
normal	On a **normal** Friday night, Sandra liked to go to the movies with her friends.	The surprise ending of the play was **unusual**. _____
location	It was hard to find the **location** on the map.	The company was looking for the perfect **place** to build a skyscraper. _____
outcome	The last play of the game determined the **outcome**.	The **beginning** of the story was sad and dreary. _____

Write the synonym

Write the vocabulary word that means almost the same as the word in parentheses.

1. **(hard)** Learning to hang glide can be _____.

2. **(regular)** It is _____ to feel nervous before you take off.

3. **(great)** When you are in the air, the distance to the ground can seem _____.

4. **(place)** Did you ever figure out the _____ of your keys?

5. **(grand)** If you are lucky, you may see the _____ flight of an eagle.

6. **(ending)** When did you learn the _____ of the election?

Write the antonym

Write the vocabulary word that means the opposite of the word in parentheses.

7. **(special)** Saturday morning is the _____ time for our football game.

8. **(easy)** It is _____ to score against that team.

9. **(beginning)** The _____ of the Senate vote was not known.

10. **(tiny)** Last night's storm left an _____ puddle in the middle of the field.

11. **(ordinary)** The soccer ball sailed in a _____ arc and landed in the goal.

You've done some reading about challenging sports. Now write some sentences about them.

Show that you know

Write sentences using at least three of the words from the box.

| challenging | outcome | immense |
| normal | location | majestic |

12.

13.

14.

READ on your OWN
Sports on the Edge, pages 23–25

BEFORE YOU READ

Think about the last pages you read in "Extreme Sports." What is one kind of safety equipment freestyle riders wear?

AS YOU READ

Read page 23 of "Big Wave Surfing." (STOP)
Fill in that part of the chart below.

Read "Tow-in Surfers," pages 24–25. (STOP)
Fill in that part of the chart.

VOCABULARY
Watch for the words you are learning about.

locate: look for and find

method: way or plan of doing something

outcome: the way something turns out

majestic: very impressive

FLUENCY
Remember to read smoothly. Try to read phrases instead of individual words.

Big Wave Surfing	Tow-in Surfers
Main idea	**Main idea**
Important details	**Important details**

AFTER YOU READ

Which extreme sport seems more dangerous to you, BMX biking or surfing the big waves? Why?

↓ SUMMARIZE: Write a Summary

How to Summarize

Step 1
Identify the **topic**. Ask, *Who or what is this about?*

Step 2
Identify the **main idea**. Ask, *What is the main thing the writer is saying about the topic?*

Step 3
Identify the **important details**. Ask, *What details are needed to understand the main idea?*

Step 4
Use the main idea and important details to **summarize**.

Learn the STRATEGY

You have practiced identifying the topic, main idea, and important details. Now you're ready for the next step, which is writing your own **summary**.

When you summarize, you briefly state the main idea of a paragraph or passage in your own words. You also include the important details. Think to yourself, *What would I tell a friend about what I just read?*

Below is a passage with two paragraphs. The main idea of the first paragraph is that the hang glider is like a kite but has a more complicated design. A good summary might be like the following:

> A hang glider is like a kite but has a more complicated design. The pilot is strapped into a harness beneath the glider.

A hang glider is a carefully designed aircraft. It is flown by a pilot. It may look like a kite, but it's much more complicated. A hang glider has a harness and a control bar. The pilot is strapped into the harness and hangs underneath the hang glider. The harness isn't really comfortable.

To steer the hang glider, the pilot holds onto the control bar and leans to either side. The pilot can also push the control bar forward or backward to change the speed. Changing speed is fun.

Read the second paragraph of the passage. Write the **main idea**.

_____

_____

Write a **summary** of the second paragraph.

_____

_____

_____

_____

Now write a brief **summary** of the whole passage by combining the summaries of the two paragraphs.

_____

_____

_____

_____

_____

_____

▶YOUR TURN

Read "Getting Into the Air." Then follow the numbered directions.

Getting Into the AIR

- **1.** Write the main idea.

- **2.** Underline the most important details.
- **3.** Summarize the paragraph.

- **4.** Write the main idea.

- **5.** Underline the most important details.
- **6.** Summarize the paragraph.

Running Launches

The pilot of a hang glider does not just jump off a cliff to get into the air. The normal **method** is to launch from a running start. The best **locations** to launch from are open areas near cliffs. These places allow the pilot plenty of room to run. The pilot gets strapped into the harness of the hang glider. Then the pilot runs with the wind until he or she is flying. The launch site should also be within **range** of a safe landing site.

Towing Launches

Hang gliders can be towed into the air by a car or small plane. A car can pull the hang glider on a dolly until the wind picks it up. A very small, light plane can also pull the hang glider into the air. Then the tow rope is dropped. The **outcome** is flight. You might think that a towing launch would be easier than a running launch. However, only experienced pilots should be towed because of the speed involved.

- **7.** Use your summary of each paragraph to complete a short summary of "Getting Into the Air." *Hang gliders get into the air by*

> **Practice reading difficult sentences until you can read and reread them smoothly.**
>
> FLUENCY

READ on your OWN
Sports on the Edge, pages 26–28

BEFORE YOU READ

Think about the last pages you read in "Extreme Sports." What makes tow-in surfing so challenging?

AS YOU READ

Read page 26 of "In-Line Insanity." (STOP)
Fill in that part of the chart below.

Read "Getting Aggressive," pages 27–28 (STOP)
Fill in that part of the chart.

VOCABULARY
Watch for the words you are learning about.

method: way of doing something

route: way to get somewhere

normal: usual, ordinary

location: place

ranging: going from one point to another

FLUENCY
Remember to think about smoothness as you read.

In-Line Insanity	*Getting Aggressive*
Main idea	**Main idea**
Important details	**Important details**
Summary	**Summary**

AFTER YOU READ

Which are more exciting in the sport of in-line skating, the tricks or the jumps? Explain your choice.

↓ SUMMARIZE: Know Your Purpose

How to Summarize

Step 1
Identify the **topic**. Ask, *Who or what is this about?*

Step 2
Identify the **main idea**. Ask, *What is the main thing the writer is saying about the topic?*

Step 3
Identify the **important details**. Ask, *What details are needed to understand the main idea?*

Step 4
Use the main idea and important details to **summarize**.

Good readers think about the reason, or purpose, for reading. Knowing the purpose helps a reader focus on important details. These details can then be used to write a summary.

When you read a comic book, you are reading to be entertained. Your focus is on the main events in the story and the main characters. If you were summarizing the comic book for a friend, you would tell about these events and characters.

When you read a textbook, your purpose is to learn information. Your focus is on important facts or ideas. These facts or ideas are the main ideas and important details you use to write your summary.

The passage below is about the history of flight and the Wright brothers. Before you read it, decide your purpose for reading and write it in the side column.

My purpose for reading is _____
_____
_____
_____

As you read the passage, underline **important details**. Then write a **summary** of the passage.

_____
_____
_____
_____
_____

The Wright brothers made their first flight in 1903 in a plane powered by an engine. The airplane they flew had two propellers. It also had a small gas engine. The longest flight lasted almost a minute. For 2 more years, they worked to solve the problems they had with the first flight. They made Kitty Hawk, North Carolina, famous by testing their airplanes. Finally, in 1905, they made a flight that lasted over half an hour. The airplane flew a distance of around 25 miles.

YOUR TURN

As you read the "The Forces of Flying," think about your purpose for reading. Then follow the numbered directions.

SCIENCE CONNECTION

The Forces of Flying

Four powerful forces make flight possible. These forces are gravity, lift, thrust, and drag. Gravity is the force that pulls things toward the ground, and lift is the force that pushes things up. These two forces are opposites. Thrust and drag also do opposite things. Thrust pushes things forward, and drag holds them back.

An airplane's engines create thrust, and this pushes the airplane forward. As the plane moves faster and faster, the air pressure under the wings lifts the plane into the air. This is the force of lift. Thrust and lift work against the forces of drag and gravity. The **outcome** is flight.

When an airplane slows down, the forces of gravity and drag start to become stronger. The **method** used to land an airplane is to slow the engines. As the engines slow down, the force of thrust decreases. Then the forces of drag and gravity come into play. Drag slows the airplane, and gravity pulls the airplane toward the ground.

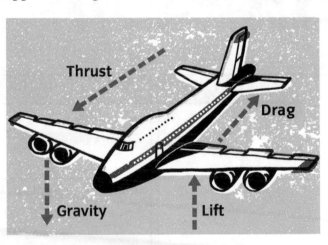

Thrust · **Drag** · **Gravity** · **Lift**

1. State a purpose for reading this passage.

2. Underline important details in the passage.

3. Summarize the passage.

> Scan the passage for unfamiliar words and look them up before you read. Knowing what the words mean will help you read more smoothly.
>
> *FLUENCY*

READ on your OWN
Sports on the Edge, pages 29–31

BEFORE YOU READ

Think about the last pages you read in "Extreme Sports." How are in-line skates different from roller skates?

AS YOU READ

Read "Being the Best," pages 29–31. (STOP)
Fill in that part of the chart below.

Read "What's Next?" page 31. (STOP)
Fill in that part of the chart.

VOCABULARY

Watch for the words you are learning about.

outcome: the way something turns out

FLUENCY

Remember to look up the meanings of unfamiliar words before you read.

Being the Best	What's Next?
Main idea	**Main idea**
Important details	**Important details**
Summary	**Summary**

AFTER YOU READ

Imagine you were asked to invent a new sport. What would it be?

Make Words Yours!

Learn the WORDS

Here are some words you will be reading in the next weeks. They are also words you need to know for your everyday reading.

WORD AND EXPLANATION	EXAMPLE	WRITE AN EXAMPLE
If something is **constant**, it happens all the time or never stops.	Mom was annoyed by the **constant** dripping of the faucet.	What noise might you describe as **constant**?
Despite means in spite of or without worrying about what will happen.	You might decide to try an extreme sport **despite** its dangers.	What else might you decide to do **despite** your fears?
To **occur** means to happen.	Unusual things **occur** every day.	What is something that **occurs** every year?
Something that is **positive** is sure or certain. It can also be helpful or constructive.	Tami's **positive** attitude helped her learn to snowboard quickly.	Why is a **positive** attitude good?
When you **predict**, you say what you think will happen. You use what's happened in the past to help you **predict** the future.	When you see dark clouds overhead, you can **predict** rain.	Who might **predict** the weather?
Something **previous** was earlier, or came before.	Our team won ten games in the **previous** season.	What did your science class study during the **previous** month?
If you **react** to something that happens, you respond to it in some way.	How did Micah **react** to the good news?	How might you **react** to getting an *A* on a test?
Something that is a **tradition** is a custom, idea, or belief that is handed down.	Our family has a **tradition** of eating Sunday dinner together.	What is one of your school's **traditions**?

YOUR TURN

Answer these questions and be ready to explain your answers.

1. Do you *react* quickly when you are tired? _____

2. If you did something *despite* being afraid, would you be proud of yourself? _____

3. If you are *positive* that you are right about something, should you say so? _____

4. If a *constant* rain is falling, do you need an umbrella? _____

Choose the right word

> tradition   despite   react   predict
> constant   occur   positive   previous

Fill each blank with the correct word from the box.

5. I didn't know how to _____ to Jared's news.

6. We finished the game _____ the rain.

7. It's a _____ to stand during "The Star-Spangled Banner."

8. I _____ that you will do very well on the test.

9. Our dog's _____ barking upsets the neighbors.

10. I wonder what will _____ at the awards ceremony tomorrow night.

11. Are you _____ that you don't want pizza?

12. My bike was painted by its _____ owner.

You've probably been to sporting events or seen them on TV. Finish these sentences to show what you know about sports.

Show that you know

Complete the sentences.

13. A sports team might have a *tradition* of _____

14. If a team won all of its *previous* games, you might *predict* that _____

15. Some sports that *occur* in the summer are _____

READ on your OWN
Sports on the Edge, pages 32–35

BEFORE YOU READ

Think about what you know about unusual moments in sports.
What unusual moments in sports have you seen in person or on TV?

AS YOU READ

Read "What's So Unusual About That?" pages 32–34. (STOP)
Fill in that part of the chart below.

Read page 35 of "Strike Up the Band." (STOP)
Fill in that part of the chart.

VOCABULARY
Watch for the words you are learning about.

predict: say what you think will happen

occur: happen

tradition: custom

react: respond to something

positive: sure

FLUENCY
Practice reading a paragraph until you can read it smoothly and without mistakes.

What's So Unusual About That?	Strike Up the Band
Main idea	Main idea
Important details	Important details
Summary	Summary

AFTER YOU READ

Which sport do you think has the most thrilling comebacks or twists?

SUMMARIZE: Use Headings

How to Summarize

Step 1
Identify the **topic**. Ask, *Who or what is this about?*

Step 2
Identify the **main idea**. Ask, *What is the main thing the writer is saying about the topic?*

Step 3
Identify the **important details**. Ask, *What details are needed to understand the main idea?*

Step 4
Use the main idea and important details to **summarize**.

Learn the STRATEGY

Chapter **titles** and **headings** can be a big help when you are summarizing. They can help you identify topics. They can help you organize your thinking, figure out main ideas, and remember important details.

Sometimes you can write a short summary of an entire selection by using just the chapter title and headings.

What is the **topic** of Chapter 2?

a. biking basics
b. what a BMX bike is
c. where to find BMX bikes

Choose the best **summary** of the chapter.

a. Learning the rules of the road is the most important part of learning to ride a bike safely.
b. Bicycling involves finding the right bike, wearing safety gear, and learning the rules of the road.
c. Learning to ride a bike is very difficult, takes many hours of training, and should be done with safety gear.

YOUR TURN

Comprehension/Vocabulary/Fluency

**Read "BMX Biking."
Then follow the numbered
directions.**

BMX Biking

1. Circle the title and headings.

2. What is the topic?

BMX stands for bicycle motocross. (The *X* stands for *cross*.) BMX bikers race on dirt tracks. Their bikes are smaller and lighter than normal bikes. This makes it easier for bikers to do tricks.

The Tricks

3. Underline the sentence that identifies the main idea of this section.

Riders start with basic tricks. One trick every rider learns is the wheelie. To do a wheelie, a biker rides on just the back wheel. Another trick is the bunny hop. To do a bunny hop, a biker gets both wheels off the ground. This trick lets riders hop up stairs and onto curbs.

It is a **tradition** for new BMX bikers to learn a trick called the curb endo. *Endo* is short for "end-over-end." When a curb endo is done correctly, a biker rides into a curb. Then the rider makes the bike's back end pop up over its front end.

Safety Gear

Despite many hours of practice, accidents happen. If a trick doesn't go right, bikers don't have much time to **react**. It's difficult to **predict** exactly what the bike will do. That's why BMX bikers know that wearing safety gear, such as helmets and knee pads, is especially important!

4. Underline the sentence that identifies the main idea of this section.

5. Use the title, headings, and the main-idea sentences to write a summary of the passage.

Reread the passage with expression. Pretend you are reading to someone who knows nothing about BMX biking.

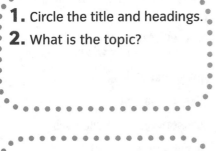

FLUENCY

READ on your OWN
Sports on the Edge, pages 36–39

BEFORE YOU READ

Think about the last pages you read in "Unusual Moments in Sports."
Why do people watch sports in person or on TV?

AS YOU READ

Read "Rivals," pages 36–38. (STOP)
Fill in that part of the chart below.

Read "'The Play,'" pages 38–39. (STOP)
Fill in that part of the chart.

VOCABULARY
Watch for the words you are learning about.

tradition: custom

constant: happening again and again

unpredictable: not possible to say what you think will happen

previous: earlier

despite: in spite of

constantly: again and again

occurred: happened

FLUENCY
Practice reading with expression.

Rivals	*'The Play'*
Main idea	**Main idea**
Important details	**Important details**
Summary	**Summary**

AFTER YOU READ

What part of the 1982 game between the California Bears and the
Stanford Cardinal seemed most unusual to you?

Get Wordwise!
The Suffixes *-ion* and *-able*

Learn More About the WORDS

You know that a **suffix** is a word part added to the end of a word to change its meaning slightly.

The suffix *-ion* means the result of an act or process. Adding *-ion* to a verb forms a noun.

react + ion = react<u>ion</u>

The suffix *-able* means possible to. Adding *-able* to a verb forms an adjective.

predict + able = predict<u>able</u>

WORD IN CONTEXT	ADD *-ion* TO THE WORD	WRITE AN EXAMPLE
Weather people try to **predict** when it will snow.	Marta's _____ about the outcome of the game was correct.	What is a **prediction** you've made?
John tried not to **react** when he heard the bad news.	Zack had a very positive _____ to the news.	What is one **reaction** to good news?
It would be hard to **locate** your home from an airplane.	Drop the *e* in **locate** before you add the suffix. That's a great _____ for the new stadium.	If you could change the **location** of your locker, where would it be?

WORD IN CONTEXT	ADD *-able* TO THE WORD	WRITE AN EXAMPLE
I **predict** that Tia will win because her painting is so pretty.	His behavior is so _____.	What is **predictable** in your day?
The book was so big that it was easy to **locate** on the shelf.	Drop the *e* in **locate** before you add the suffix. Would a white T-shirt be _____ in the snow?	What would be easily **locatable** in a classroom?

→YOUR TURN

Choose the right word

predictable   reaction   prediction   locatable

Fill in the blanks with the best word from the box.

1. Would you like to make a [_____] about who will win the award?

2. The street was so small it wasn't [_____] on a map.

3. That was a very [_____] response.

4. Tamika knew Jimmy was surprised because of his [_____].

Which word works?

Circle the correct word in each pair.

5. I couldn't **locate / location** my name on that list.

6. The park is the perfect **locate / location** for the festival.

7. How would you **react / reaction** if an Olympic star came to your school?

8. Would everyone's **react / reaction** be the same?

9. It's hard to **predict / prediction** what will happen.

10. His silly **predict / prediction** made me laugh.

11. Can someone **locate / locatable** the restaurant's phone number?

12. The phone numbers for most businesses are **locate / locatable** in the Yellow Pages.

You have probably seen some unusual moments in sports. Use words with the suffix *-ion* or *-able* to write about them.

Show that you know

Write sentences using at least two words from the box at the top of the page.

13.

14.

READ on your OWN
Sports on the Edge, pages 40–42

BEFORE YOU READ

Think about the last pages you read in "Unusual Moments in Sports." What was so amusing about the college football game between the Stanford Cardinal and the California Bears in 1982?

AS YOU READ

Read page 40 of "The Vault." (STOP)
Fill in that part of the chart below.

Read "World Rivals," pages 40–42. (STOP)
Fill in that part of the chart.

VOCABULARY
Watch for the words you are learning about.

occur: happen

constant: happening again and again

previous: earlier

despite: in spite of

FLUENCY
To help you read with expression, pretend you are reading aloud to a friend.

The Vault	*World Rivals*
Main idea	**Main idea**
Important details	**Important details**
Summary	**Summary**

AFTER YOU READ

What is the most surprising thing you learned about gymnastics on these pages?

↓ SUMMARIZE: Use Lists

How to Summarize

Step 1
Identify the **topic**. Ask, *Who or what is this about?*

Step 2
Identify the **main idea**. Ask, *What is the main thing the writer is saying about the topic?*

Step 3
Identify the **important details**. Ask, *What details are needed to understand the main idea?*

Step 4
Use the main idea and important details to **summarize**.

Learn the STRATEGY

Writing a summary, as you've learned, involves stating the main idea and important details. **Lists** can help you do this.

You will often come across lists in your reading. When you see a list, think about what the items in the list all have in common. Sometimes the items on a list all relate to the main idea. Often, they are important details.

For example, what do apples, oranges, and bananas have in common? Of course, they are all fruits. Knowing that they are all fruits might help you summarize a paragraph or passage in which the list appears.

Bikers have developed their own language. They talk about diggers, biffs, buzzes, and gonzos.

Diggers and Biffs Mountain bikers ride in dangerous places. Hitting a rock, riding over a tree root, and skidding on loose gravel can all happen to a biker. They might even send the biker headfirst into the ground. Bikers call this a digger or face plant. Crashing into something is called a biff.

Buzzes and Gonzos A buzz is the thrill that bikers feel after a successful climb. Buzzes make up for the biffs and diggers. Surviving something extreme, or gonzo, gives bikers an especially satisfying buzz.

In the passage, circle the **list** that can be summed up as *words that bikers use*.

What do hitting a rock, riding over a tree root, and skidding on loose gravel have in common?

a. They make mountain biking fun.

b. They cause accidents.

c. They are tricks.

Write a **summary** of the passage.

_____

_____

_____

_____

Read "The Road to Mountain Bikes." Then follow the numbered directions.

The Road to Mountain BIKES

1. Circle the list in the first paragraph.

2. Write the main idea of each section.

Oops!:

Better but Not Best:

From Flat to Fat:

3. What do logs, rocks, loose gravel, and rough, steep hills have in common?

4. Write a summary of "The Road to Mountain Bikes."

When you look at a modern mountain bike, you see a machine designed for speed, control, and safety. This bike wasn't invented overnight. It was the outcome of more than a hundred years of changes.

Oops! The first bicycles were invented in the late 1700s as a method of transportation. However, traveling on one of these bikes was dangerous! Many accidents would **occur** because the front wheel was much larger than the back wheel. The difference in wheel size made the bike hard to control. Riding downhill put you in **constant** danger of falling off headfirst.

Better but Not Best Then, in the late 1800s, a bike with same-size wheels was created. With these safer bikes, people started to race. People raced on flat roads and tracks. The bicycles didn't handle well over obstacles, though.

From Flat to Fat In the 1970s, people began putting fatter tires on their bikes. These bikes could travel over uneven surfaces much better than **previous** bicycles. Another **positive** feature was the addition of shock absorbers. These shocks provided good traction and control. The new bikes allowed riders to ride over logs and rocks, through loose gravel, and down rough, steep hills. Riders didn't have to fall off to stop!

As you read, vary your volume to make the reading interesting.

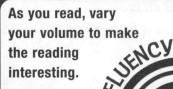

READ on your OWN
Sports on the Edge, pages 43–45

BEFORE YOU READ

Think about the last pages you read in "Unusual Moments in Sports." Why was 1972 a turning point in women's gymnastics and 1984 a turning point for American women's gymnastics?

AS YOU READ

Read "The Competition," pages 43–45. (STOP)
Fill in the chart below.

The Competition
Main idea
Important details
Summary

VOCABULARY
Watch for the words you are learning about.

previous: earlier

predicted: said what you thought would happen in the future

positive: sure

despite: in spite of

FLUENCY
Vary your volume to make your reading interesting.

AFTER YOU READ

If you were the coach, would you have let Strug compete on an injured ankle? Why or why not?

SUMMARIZE: Use Notes

How to Summarize

Step 1
Identify the **topic**. Ask, *Who or what is this about?*

Step 2
Identify the **main idea**. Ask, *What is the main thing the writer is saying about the topic?*

Step 3
Identify the **important details**. Ask, *What details are needed to understand the main idea?*

Step 4
Use the main idea and important details to **summarize**.

Learn the STRATEGY

You've learned to use titles and headings to help you find topics, main ideas, and important details. Did you know that you can also use these features to make notes about what you read? Then you can use the information in your notes to create a summary in your own words.

A good set of notes contains the topic of the passage, the headings, and the important details. If there are no headings in what you are reading, make up headings of your own that sum up the main ideas you read about.

Read the passage below and follow the directions in the side column.

TRICYCLES

Women's Tricycles The first tricycles were made for women. In the late 1800s, women wore long full skirts, so they could not ride the two-wheeled bicycles that men rode. The tricycle had three wheels. The seat was located between two large back wheels and the pedals were located below the seat. So women wearing skirts could sit and pedal without any problems.

Children's Tricycles Later, tricycles were made for children. The children's tricycle was simple and small enough for a young child. Like the earlier tricycle, it had three wheels. Usually, the back wheels were small and the front wheel was larger. It had a seat above the back wheels. Pedals were attached to the front wheel. Children usually learned to ride a tricycle before they learned to ride a bicycle.

Circle the title of the passage and add it to the notes below.

Underline the headings. Add them to the notes. Then, find important details to list under each heading.

Title/Topic: _____
Heading and details:
Women's Tricycles

1. _____
   _____
2. _____
   _____

Heading and details:
_____
1. _____
   _____
2. _____
   _____
3. _____
   _____

Summary of the second paragraph:
_____
_____
_____
_____
_____

➤YOUR TURN

Read "Iron Riders." Then follow the numbered directions.

Iron Riders

In 1896, the Twenty-fifth Infantry Bicycle Corps was born. The U.S. Army in Fort Missoula, Montana, wanted to test using bicycles for military purposes in mountainous areas.

Bicycle Popularity Cycling had become very popular in the 1890s. People used bicycles for transportation, sport, and recreation. European countries already used bicycles in the military. The U.S. military had **previously** used cyclists for carrying messages.

Bikes vs. Horses General Nelson A. Miles approved the request to form a bicycle corps. He thought bikes might be better than horses. He wrote that a bike did not need to be fed, watered, and rested. A bike was also smaller and quieter than a horse and could go to all kinds of locations.

The Corps' Success The Twenty-fifth Infantry was made up of African American soldiers who rode one-speed bicycles. Their first trip was 126 miles carrying 76 pounds of gear. It lasted 4 days. Other trips ranged from 790 to 1,900 miles! The soldiers traveled 56 miles a day **despite** mountainous conditions. They averaged 6.3 miles per hour. The **outcome** was **positive**. These "iron riders" proved that a bicycle unit could travel twice as fast as horses or infantry at one-third the cost.

1. Complete the notes.

Title/Topic: Iron Riders

Heading and details: _____

1. _____

2. _____

Heading and details: _____

1. _____

2. _____

3. _____

Heading and details: _____

1. _____

2. _____

2. Use your notes to write a summary.

> Avoid reading in a monotone, even if the passage is informational.

FLUENCY

READ on your OWN
Sports on the Edge, pages 46–48

BEFORE YOU READ

Think about the last pages you read in "Unusual Moments in Sports." Why did Bela Karolyi carry Kerri Strug when the team accepted the gold medal at the 1996 Olympics?

AS YOU READ

Read page 46 of "Williams Versus Williams." (STOP)
Fill in the important details in the notes below.

Read "From Althea Gibson to the Williams Sisters," page 47. (STOP)
Fill in the notes.

Read "The Williams Sisters Grow Up," page 48. (STOP)
Fill in the notes.

Williams Versus Williams	From Althea Gibson to the Williams Sisters	The Williams Sisters Grow Up
Heading and details: The U.S. Open	Heading and details: Althea Gibson's impact	Heading and details: Growing up

AFTER YOU READ

Is tennis a sport you would like to play? Why or why not?

VOCABULARY
Watch for the words you are learning about.

constant: continued

positive: sure of

previously: formerly

FLUENCY
Avoid reading in a monotone. Vary expression whether the passage is lighthearted, informational, or conversational.

Make Words Yours!

Learn the WORDS

Here are eight more words you'll need to know as you read about unusual moments in sports. You'll also need these words for your everyday reading.

WORD AND EXPLANATION	EXAMPLE	WRITE AN EXAMPLE
A **contrast** is a difference. When you **contrast** two things, you show how they are different.	A **contrast** in the brothers' activities is that one jogs daily and the other doesn't.	What is one **contrast** between you and your best friend?
An **error** is a mistake.	The catcher made an **error** behind home plate.	What kind of **errors** are easy to correct?
When you **focus** on something, you concentrate on it and block everything else out.	It's important for students to **focus** on their studies.	What is your main **focus** outside school?
An **impact** happens when one thing hits against another. An **impact** is also the effect that something has.	Juan's positive attitude has had a great **impact** on the other players.	Who has had an **impact** on your life?
When you **maintain** something, you keep it as it already is.	Eating the right foods will help you **maintain** good health.	What can you do to **maintain** a positive attitude?
To **proceed** means to move forward or to continue, sometimes after a short pause.	I'm back, so you may **proceed** with your story.	How would you **proceed** if someone interrupted your joke?
If you **remove** something, you take it away or take it off.	Pat's mother asked him to **remove** his muddy shoes before he entered the house.	When should you **remove** your hat from your head?
A **series** is a group of related things that come one after the other.	The losing team made a **series** of costly mistakes.	What sporting events are played in a **series**?

→ YOUR TURN

Yes or No?

Answer these questions and be ready to explain your answers.

1. Should players *focus* and *maintain* their composure during a game no matter what happens? _____

2. Could one *error* have an *impact* on the outcome of a game? _____

Choose the right word

```
contrast   proceed   remove   series
error      focus      impact   maintain
```

Fill each blank with the correct word from the box.

3. Tanya did a [_____] of flips in her gymnastics routine.

4. I will [_____] to basketball practice after school.

5. I will [_____] my jacket when it gets warmer.

6. In [_____] to some of the other players, Luis is a star.

7. The [_____] of the ball broke the bat.

8. The scientist had to [_____] on his experiment for months.

9. Juan was able to [_____] his concentration despite the noise.

10. I was very upset because my [_____] cost the team the game.

You probably have some opinions about sports. Show that you know the words by writing about your opinions.

Show that you know

Answer the questions. Use sentences.

11. How would you *contrast* two of your favorite athletes?

12. Why might an injured athlete want to *proceed* to play in a game?

13. Why might a referee *remove* a player from a game?

14. Should teams play a *series* of games or one game to decide which team is better? Why?

READ on your OWN
Sports on the Edge, pages 49–51

BEFORE YOU READ

Think about the last pages you read in "Unusual Moments in Sports." Why was Althea Gibson important to the Williams sisters?

AS YOU READ

Read "The Williams Sisters Rise to the Top," pages 49–50. (STOP)
Fill in the important details and summarize in the chart below.

Read "An All-Williams Final," pages 50–51. (STOP)
Fill in the details and summarize in the chart.

VOCABULARY
Watch for the words you are learning about.

proceeded: moved forward or continued

contrast: compare the differences

maintained: kept

FLUENCY
Practice using tone to add emotion to your reading.

The Williams Sisters Rise to the Top	An All-Williams Final
Heading and details: Sisters turn professional	**Heading and details:** Sisters meet in the U.S. Open final
Summary	**Summary**

AFTER YOU READ

How would you feel if you had to compete against your best friend?

SUMMARIZE: Review the Steps

How to Summarize

Step 1
Identify the **topic**. Ask, *Who or what is this about?*

Step 2
Identify the **main idea**. Ask, *What is the main thing the writer is saying about the topic?*

Step 3
Identify the **important details**. Ask, *What details are needed to understand the main idea?*

Step 4
Use the main idea and important details to **summarize**.

Learn the STRATEGY

In this unit, you have learned how and why you should summarize. Summarizing is useful because it helps you understand and remember what you read, whether what you read is a textbook, a newspaper article, or a story. To help you summarize, you have learned how to

- identify the **topic**.
- identify the **main idea**.
- identify the **important details**.

Kelly was a skateboarder, but he had never tried snowboarding before. He was nervous as he stood at the top of the mountain. He put on his helmet and strapped on the wrist guards he always wore because he had broken his wrist skateboarding when he was 10 years old. He clicked his boots onto the board and faced downhill. He took a deep breath, pressed his toes forward, and started down. When he thought he was moving a bit too fast, he pulled his toes up and leaned more on his heels. As a result, he slowed down. *This is easy*, he thought. *It's just like skateboarding!*

What is the **topic** of this passage?

_____

_____

What is the **main idea**?

_____

_____

_____

Underline **important details** in this passage.

Write a brief **summary** of the passage.

_____

_____

_____

_____

_____

_____

YOUR TURN

Read "TV Tumble." Then follow the numbered directions.

1. What is the topic of this passage?

2. What is the main idea of the passage?

3. Underline the important details in the passage.

4. Write a summary of the passage.

TV TUMBLE

Even professional snowboarders fall sometimes. Just ask Tara Dakides. Dakides is one of the world's best snowboarders. She has won five gold medals at the X Games, in **contrast** to other female snowboarders. In 2004, she was performing on David Letterman's television show when something unusual happened. Dakides was going to do snowboarding stunts outside, so the TV crew set up a special ramp in the middle of the street and covered it with snow. In the afternoon, she practiced a **series** of jumps. Then, she rested backstage. Finally, it was time for the show.

Dakides **proceeded** as usual with her first two jumps. Then on her third jump, she attacked the hill the same way she had all day, but her snowboard slipped. Unfortunately for Dakides, the snow had begun to melt, which made the jump almost impossible to complete. Dakides fell 15 feet onto the street. As a result, she had to get stitches in her head. Still, Dakides wasn't going to let this accident stop her. Before the stitches were **removed**, she went on Letterman's show again and joked with him about her scary fall.

Read the passage aloud at a comfortable pace. Reread the passage until you can read it quickly and without mistakes.

FLUENCY

READ on your OWN
Sports on the Edge, pages 52–54

BEFORE YOU READ

Think about the last pages you read in "Unusual Moments in Sports." What unusual event happened in the 2001 U.S. Open final?

AS YOU READ

Read page 52 of "Foul Play?" (STOP)
Fill in that part of the chart below.

Read "The Billy Goat Curse?" pages 53–54. (STOP)
Fill in that part of the chart.

VOCABULARY
Watch for the words you are learning about.

series: the World Series in baseball is a group of seven games to determine the champion

removed: took something away

error: mistake

FLUENCY
If you find yourself reading so quickly that you are missing the meaning, slow down.

Foul Play?	*The Billy Goat Curse?*
Main idea	**Main idea**
Important details	**Important details**
Summary	**Summary**

AFTER YOU READ

Do you think the Billy Goat Curse was the real reason the Cubs lost the game? Why or why not?

Get Wordwise!
Noun or Verb?

Learn More About the WORDS

A **noun** is a word that names a person, place, thing, or idea.

A **verb** is a word that shows action.

Many words can be used as both nouns and verbs. A word's meaning as a noun is slightly different from its meaning as a verb.

Look at the chart and think about how the words are used. Then fill in the missing parts.

WORD	USED AS A NOUN	USED AS A VERB
impact	**Meaning:** one thing hitting another; the effect that something has on a person **Example:** The decision had a big **impact** on our lives.	**Meaning:** to have an effect on **Example:** The decision **impacted** our lives.
focus	**Meaning:** the center of attention **Write an example:**	**Meaning:** to concentrate on something **Example:** Jim **focused** his attention on the coach's speech.
contrast	**Meaning:** difference **Write an example:**	**Meaning:** to show how things are different **Example:** She **contrasted** the two options available to her.
challenge	**Meaning:** something that takes hard work **Example:** Running a 5K race is quite a **challenge**.	**Meaning:** to invite or dare someone to take part in a contest or something difficult **Write an example:**
feature	**Meaning:** the main point or highlight **Example:** The plan for the new stadium has some interesting **features**.	**Meaning:** to focus on something and make it special **Write an example:**

→YOUR TURN

Noun or Verb?

Read each sentence and think about how the underlined word is used. Write *noun* or *verb* on the line.

1. The coach's challenge was to motivate the players. _____

2. Today's sports section featured an article on the football game. _____

3. The best athletes focus their attention during games. _____

4. The star player's retirement impacted the entire sports world. _____

5. The contrast in the tennis players' styles was great. _____

> Show that you know nouns and verbs by answering questions about sports.

Now you try it

Rewrite each sentence without using the underlined word. The first is done for you.

6. Carly was the focus of an article on Olympic gymnasts.
   An article on Olympic gymnasts was mainly about Carly.

7. Josh challenged his sister to arm wrestle. _____ _____

8. The fans compared and contrasted their favorite players. _____ _____

9. The magazine featured other Olympic athletes, too. _____ _____

10. Susie's kindness had an impact on her friends. _____ _____

Show that you know

Answer the questions. Use sentences.

11. What is one *challenge* in playing a sport? _____

12. What would you do if someone *challenged* you to play an unfamiliar sport? _____

READ on your OWN
Sports on the Edge, pages 55–57

BEFORE YOU READ

Think about the last pages you read in "Unusual Moments in Sports."
How did the Chicago Cubs fans try to end the Billy Goat Curse?

AS YOU READ

Read page 55 of "The Best." (STOP)
Fill in that part of the chart below.

Read "A Love of the Game," pages 56–57. (STOP)
Fill in that part of the chart.

VOCABULARY
Watch for the words you are learning about.

impact: effect

maintain: remain the same

FLUENCY
Read at an appropriate pace. Practice until you can read quickly without mistakes.

The Best	A Love of the Game
Main idea	**Main idea**
Important details	**Important details**
Summary	**Summary**

AFTER YOU READ

Choose the most interesting thing you learned about Michael Jordan in the chapter and write about what you learned.

SUMMARIZE: In Your Own Words

How to Summarize

Step 1
Identify the **topic**. Ask, *Who or what is this about?*

Step 2
Identify the **main idea**. Ask, *What is the main thing the writer is saying about the topic?*

Step 3
Identify the **important details**. Ask, *What details are needed to understand the main idea?*

Step 4
Use the main idea and important details to **summarize**.

Learn the STRATEGY

A **summary** is a brief description of what you read in your own words. Your summary should include the main idea of what you read followed by the most important details. To help you write your summary, here are some things you can do or be on the lookout for as you read:

- **Know your purpose** for reading, which means setting a reading goal for yourself. Previewing the text for clues can help you set your purpose.
- Use **titles and headings** to preview the text and organize your thinking.
- Note **lists** in the text that may provide clues to important points.
- Make **notes** on a paragraph or section.

When you go surfing, two big forces are at work—gravity and buoyancy.

Gravity Gravity is the force of attraction between two objects. Gravity is what makes a fly ball in baseball come back down. Gravity is also what pulls you and your surfboard down toward the water, just as it pulls that fly ball to the ground.

Buoyancy What keeps you from sinking? A force called buoyancy pushes up on the surfboard. Buoyancy is the force that makes things float. The force of buoyancy opposes the force of gravity.

Before you read, decide on your **purpose** for reading the passage.

My purpose for reading is _____

_____

_____

As you read, underline **important details**. Then write a **summary** of the passage.

_____

_____

_____

_____

_____

_____

YOUR TURN

Read "Surfing Forces." Then follow the numbered directions

Surfing Forces

What other forces besides gravity and buoyancy are needed to surf a wave? Without forward motion and steering, a person would just float in one place.

Forward Motion When a good wave moves toward the shore, surfers start paddling with their hands. As they paddle, they push on the water. The water is pushing back, but the surfers are pushing with more force than the water. That's why they move forward. As they gain speed, they can stand up. Buoyancy is keeping them on top of the water. The moving water is pushing them forward. Now all surfers need to do is **maintain** their balance.

Steering When the wave gets as high as it will get, it starts to break. Gravity pulls the rising water back down. If surfers just follow the wave, they will go straight down with the water. The **impact** their bodies make when they hit the water at this angle is painful! Surfers need to turn to avoid the breaking water. They shift their weight onto their right foot, causing the board to turn right. This avoids the breaking wave.

If a surfer makes an **error**, the forces of nature will win, and the surfer will fall. If the surfer can **focus** on putting the correct forces on the surfboard, that surfer can ride a wave to the end.

1. Write the main idea of the section.

2. Write the main idea of the section.

3. Summarize the passage.

Read in a smooth, relaxed manner, as if you were talking in conversation.

FLUENCY

READ on your OWN
Sports on the Edge, pages 58–60

BEFORE YOU READ

Think about the last pages you read in "Unusual Moments in Sports."
What are some of Michael Jordan's achievements?

AS YOU READ

Read "Reliving a Childhood Dream," pages 58–60. (STOP)
Fill in the chart below.

Reliving a Childhood Dream
Topic
Main idea
Important details
Summary

VOCABULARY
Watch for the words you are learning about.

error: mistake

contrast: compare differences

maintained: kept

focus: concentration

FLUENCY
Everyone reads at a different pace. Practice until you can read at a pace that is comfortable for you.

AFTER YOU READ

Of all the stories you have read in "Unusual Moments in Sports," which one did you think was the most unusual or the most exciting?

Unit 1 Reflection

VOCABULARY

The easiest part of learning new words is

The hardest part is

I still need to work on

Sports on the Edge

COMPREHENSION

One way summarizing helped me with reading is

The hardest thing about summarizing is

I still need to work on

FLUENCY

I read most fluently when

I still need to work on

INDEPENDENT READING

My favorite part of <u>Sports on the Edge</u> is

COLOSSAL CONSTRUCTIONS

COMPREHENSION
LEARN WHY ASKING QUESTIONS HELPS YOU UNDERSTAND WHAT YOU READ

INDEPENDENT READING
Colossal Constructions
Includes "The Power of Pyramids" and "Superscrapers"

unit 2

Br

VOCABULARY

WORDS:
Know them!
Use them!
Learn all about them!

FLUENCY
Make your reading smooth and accurate, one tip at a time.

Make Words Yours!

Learn the WORDS

Here are some words you will be reading in the next weeks. They are also words you need to know for your everyday reading.

WORD AND EXPLANATION	EXAMPLE	WRITE AN EXAMPLE
An **architect** is someone who plans or designs buildings.	The **architects** designed a new building downtown.	If you were an **architect**, what kind of building would you design?
Something that is **confining** feels small, tight, and often uncomfortable.	The tall man found the small car to be **confining**.	What types of places do you feel are **confining**?
To **consume** means to eat or use up something.	The forest fire **consumed** trees, shrubs, and grass as it spread.	Which foods have you **consumed** in the past two days?
Destructive describes something or someone that harms people or property.	The town had to be rebuilt after the **destructive** hurricane.	How can people be **destructive**?
Something **immovable** can't be moved or relocated. The opposite of **immovable** is *movable*.	The fallen tree across the trail was **immovable** so we had to go around it.	What do you see in the room that can be described as **immovable**?
Someone with **leadership** is able to lead or give guidance and direction to a group of people.	Our class president's **leadership** helps us get things done.	Whom do you know who shows **leadership**?
A **realm** is an area. It can be a kingdom or a special area of interest.	The knight was respected throughout the **realm**.	What is your favorite topic to study in the **realm** of science?
A **tomb** is the burial place for a dead person.	The queen's **tomb** had golden doors and walls of marble.	What else might be used to mark or build a **tomb**?

⟶ YOUR TURN

True or False?

Write *true* or *false* and be ready to explain your answers.

1. *Destructive* storms can knock down trees. _____

2. An *immovable* object can be pushed out of the way. _____

3. You can visit a *tomb*. _____

4. *Leadership* is a sign of weakness. _____

Choose the right word

architects	tomb	realm	destructive
immovable	leadership	confining	consume

Fill each blank with the word from the box that best fits the description.

5. The dog is no longer hungry, and the roast is missing. _____

6. Ling has great ideas and knows how to take charge. _____

7. The kingdom stretched from sea to sea. _____

8. The storm uprooted large trees and broke windows. _____

9. People visited the place where the king was buried. _____

10. Everyone pushed, but the beached whale didn't budge. _____

11. My shoes are squeezing my feet and pinching my toes. _____

12. The team revealed its design for the new bank building. _____

Okay, now you know more about the words. Show it by writing about buildings.

Show that you know

Complete the sentences.

13. The ruler of a *realm* might build a large _____

_____

14. Buildings feel *confining* when _____

_____

15. If a building is *consumed* by fire _____

_____

16. *Architects* design large buildings so that _____

_____

READ on your OWN
Colossal Constructions, pages 3–6

BEFORE YOU READ

Think about what you already know about pyramids. Why do you think pyramids were built?

AS YOU READ

Read "What Is a Pyramid?" pages 3–5. (STOP)
Fill in the idea web below.

Read "An Afterlife Fit for a King," page 6. (STOP)
Write the answer to the question below.

VOCABULARY
Watch for the words you are learning about.

architects: people who design buildings

architectural: describing a style of building

tomb: a burial place for a dead person

confined: limited to

destruction: the condition of being damaged or destroyed

realm: a particular area, often a kingdom

FLUENCY
Use commas and periods as guides for when to pause during reading.

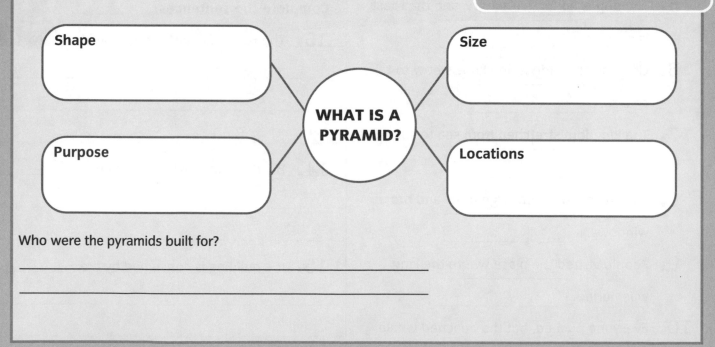

Shape

Size

WHAT IS A PYRAMID?

Purpose

Locations

Who were the pyramids built for?

_____

_____

AFTER YOU READ

Choose the section you found most interesting. What is one new fact you learned?

⬇ ASK QUESTIONS: Previewing

Kinds of Questions

Goal-Setting
Ask, *What is my reason for reading this text?*

Question Words
Ask, *What important details can I find in the text?*

Between the Lines
Ask, *What decisions can I make about the facts and details in the text?*

Beyond the Text
Ask, *What connections can I make between the text and my life?*

Learn the STRATEGY

Asking yourself questions will help you get the most out of what you read. Questions such as *What do I think this chapter will be about?* and *What will I learn?* will help you set a goal before you read. Once you've set a goal, you are more likely to remember and understand what you read.

A good way to come up with a goal-setting question is to preview. Give the text a quick look. Look for clues that tell you what the text will be about. Scan for titles, headings, pictures, captions, and boldfaced words. Then ask your goal-setting question. Try to ask about something that is important to the text.

What clues can help you ask a goal-setting question for reading this newspaper article?

_____

_____

_____

Choose the best goal-setting question for reading this newspaper article.

a. Why are Top Cyberg's fans angry?

b. What are Top Cyberg's latest songs?

c. Where does Top Cyberg live?

Preview "New Look for an Ancient Shape" and answer questions 1 and 2. Then read the passage and answer question 3.

This pyramid was added to the Louvre Museum in Paris in 1989. ▼

NEW LOOK FOR AN

ANCIENT SHAPE

1. What do you expect to learn from this passage? Write a goal-setting question.

2. What clues helped you to think up your question?

A Bold Idea How do you modify a famous building without changing its look? In 1981, the president of France decided to update the Louvre Museum. He invited a Chinese American man named I. M. Pei to design a new entrance. Many French people were angry. They thought French **architects** should do the work. Even so, the president liked Pei's ideas. Pei planned an entry to the museum that would honor the past and the present. He borrowed an ancient shape from the **realm** of the pharaohs. The entry would be a pyramid shaped like a pharaoh's **tomb**. However, this pyramid would be built of glass and steel.

A Challenge to Build Pei's design was not simple to build. The pyramid was to be made of clear glass triangles. Most heavy glass is greenish in color. Glassmakers had a hard time figuring out how to make strong, thick glass that was clear. Builders and engineers had to try new techniques, too. It was not easy to create a pyramid-shaped frame that was sturdy enough to withstand **destructive** winds.

Once the pyramid was finished, it took a while for some French people to accept it. Today, however, most museum visitors agree that Pei created a design to last for the ages.

3. What answers did the passage give for your question?

Before reading, look through the sentences for words that you don't know. Find out how to pronounce them.

FLUENCY

READ on your OWN
Colossal Constructions, pages 7–9

BEFORE YOU READ

Think about the last pages you read in "The Power of Pyramids."
Why did the ancient Egyptians build pyramids?

AS YOU READ

To preview, look at headings, pictures, captions, and boldfaced words.
Preview "Making a Mummy," pages 7–8. (STOP)
Write a goal-setting question in the chart below.

Now read pages 7–8. (STOP)
Answer your question in the chart below.

Preview "Treasures for the Afterlife," page 9. (STOP)
Write a goal-setting question in the chart below.

Now read page 9. (STOP)
Answer your question in the chart below.

VOCABULARY
Watch for the words you are learning about.

destructive: having the power to damage, hurt, or destroy

leadership: guidance

confining: keeping within tight limits

realm: area

consumed: eaten up

tomb: burial chamber

immovable: impossible to move

FLUENCY
Identify words that you don't know. Find out how to pronounce them before reading.

Making a Mummy	*Treasures for the Afterlife*
Goal-setting question	**Goal-setting question**
Answer	**Answer**

AFTER YOU READ

Would you enjoy seeing Egyptian mummies in a museum? Why or why not?

Get Wordwise!
Analogies

Learn More About the WORDS

An **analogy** is a statement that links pairs of words that go together in some way. The key to understanding an analogy is figuring out how the words are related.

The words *shoes* and *socks* go together because they are both worn on your feet. The words *bread* and *sandwich* go together because one is a part of the other.

This is the way an analogy is worded.

> *Puppy* is to *dog* as *kitten* is to *cat*.

Puppy and *dog* go together for the same reason that *kitten* and *cat* go together. The first word in each pair is the name for a baby animal, and the second word is the name for that animal when it grows up.

WORD PAIR	HOW THE WORDS GO TOGETHER	KIND OF ANALOGY	COMPLETE THE ANALOGY
sweet and **sour**	The words have opposite meanings.	Antonym	**Sweet** is to **sour** as **loose** is to **confining / comfortable**.
artist and **painting**	The first is a person and the second is what that person makes.	Worker (artist) to product (painting)	**Artist** is to **painting** as **architect** is to **hammer / building**.
hair and **cut**	The first names a thing and the second tells what you do to it.	Object (hair) to action (cut)	**Hair** is to **cut** as **food** is to **spoon / consume**.
tomb and **cemetery**	The first is located in the second, which is a larger place.	Part (tomb) to whole (cemetery)	**Tomb** is to **cemetery** as **room** is to **house / window**.

→YOUR TURN

What's the connection?

Explain why the pairs of words go together.

1. *town* and *realm* _____
_____ .

2. *body* and *tomb* _____
_____ .

3. *pizza* and *consume* _____
_____ .

4. *normal* and *strange* _____
_____ .

Choose the right word

    immovable   architect   realm   physical
    challenging   mental   error

Complete each analogy with a word from the box.

5. *Mayor* is to *city* as *king* is to
   [_____] .

6. *Young* is to *old* as *easy* is to
   [_____] .

7. *Patch* is to *tear* as *correction* is to
   [_____] .

8. *Light* is to *dark* as *movable* is to
   [_____] .

9. *Author* is to *novel* as [_____]
   is to *building*.

10. *Reading* is to [_____] as
   running is to [_____] .

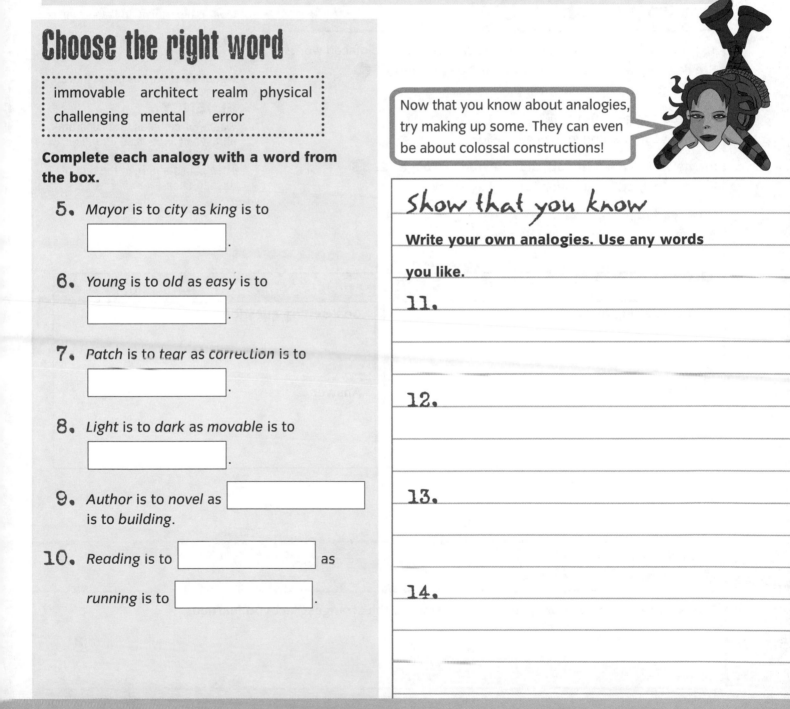

Now that you know about analogies, try making up some. They can even be about colossal constructions!

Show that you know

Write your own analogies. Use any words you like.

11. _____

12. _____

13. _____

14. _____

READ on your OWN
Colossal Constructions, pages 10–12

BEFORE YOU READ

Think about the last pages you read in "The Power of Pyramids." What kinds of objects were placed in pharaohs' tombs?

AS YOU READ

To preview, look at headings, pictures, captions, and boldfaced words.
Preview "Pyramids of Ancient Egypt," pages 10–11. (STOP)
Write a goal-setting question in the chart below.

Now read pages 10–11. (STOP)
Answer your question in the chart below.

Preview "The First Smooth-Sided Pyramid," page 12. (STOP)
Write a goal-setting question in the chart below.

Now read page 12. (STOP)
Answer your question in the chart below.

VOCABULARY
Watch for the words you are learning about.

tomb: burial chamber

realm: area

architect: a person who designs buildings

leadership: ability to lead or guide

destructive: harmful to people or property

immovable: impossible to move

FLUENCY
Watch for commas that separate phrases in sentences. Practice reading the words as a group. Then pause and read the rest of the sentence.

Pyramids of Ancient Egypt	*The First Smooth-Sided Pyramid*
Goal-setting question	**Goal-setting question**
Answer	**Answer**

AFTER YOU READ

Choose one of the sections you just read. What is the strangest fact you learned?

↓ ASK QUESTIONS: Setting a Goal

Kinds of Questions

Goal-Setting	**Question Words**	**Between the Lines**	**Beyond the Text**
Ask, *What is my reason for reading this text?*	Ask, *What important details can I find in the text?*	Ask, *What decisions can I make about the facts and details in the text?*	Ask, *What connections can I make between the text and my life?*

Learn the STRATEGY

Keeping your goal-setting question in mind as you read will help you to focus on what you're reading. As you read, check to see if the text is answering your goal-setting question. You might need to revise your question.

Ali previewed the passage below and decided on a goal-setting question. Keep his question in mind as you read the first paragraph. Then, decide if Ali should revise his question.

> What was found in the Queen's Chamber?

THE ROBOT'S DISCOVERY

The Queen's Chamber In the Great Pyramid, two shafts, or narrow tunnels, branch off from the Queen's Chamber. Scientists wondered if valuable items were hidden in the shafts. The shafts were too small for a person to crawl through, so scientists sent in a robot to do the search.

The Secret Discovery The robot made its way through one of the long shafts. When it reached the end, the robot sent back a picture. The picture showed a sealed door with metal handles. Scientists then had the robot drill through the door. It took a picture of what was on the other side. Surprisingly, it was another door. Scientists still don't know what is behind the door.

Was Ali's question answered in the passage?

_____
_____
_____
_____
_____

After reading the first paragraph, Ali revised his goal-setting question to: "What did the robot discover?" Was it a good question? Explain.

_____
_____
_____
_____

→ YOUR TURN

Preview "A Majestic Protector" and answer questions 1 and 2. Then read the passage and answer questions 3 and 4.

The Sphinx is located near the pyramid of the Egyptian pharaoh Kaphre.

A Majestic PROTECTOR

1. What clues can you use to ask a good goal-setting question?

2. What do you expect to learn from this passage? Write a goal-setting question.

The Pharaoh's Guard In the valley of Giza, a giant stone creature keeps watch. It is called the Sphinx. The Sphinx has guarded the pyramid of a pharaoh for more than 4,000 years. This **immovable** creature is the biggest statue in Egypt. It has the head of a king and the body of a lion. It is a symbol of strength and **leadership**.

The Story Stone A carved stone sits between the paws of the Sphinx. It tells this story: After the old pharaoh died, desert sands began to cover the Sphinx. It was buried up to its neck. One day Prince Tut IV fell asleep in the shade of the Sphinx. He dreamed that the Sphinx said, "Tut, dig away the **confining** sands that choke me. Do as I say and you shall be king of Egypt."

Tut awoke **consumed** by the desire to do as the Sphinx had asked. He saw to it that all of the sand was removed. Then, just as the Sphinx had promised, Tut became Egypt's next king.

3. Did the passage answer your question? Explain.

4. Did you have to revise your goal-setting question while reading? Explain.

Change your expression as you read. Speak naturally, as if you were talking to a friend.

FLUENCY

READ on your OWN
Colossal Constructions, pages 13–15

BEFORE YOU READ

Think about the last pages you read in "The Power of Pyramids."
What is the difference between a step pyramid and a smooth-sided
pyramid?

AS YOU READ

To preview, look at headings, pictures, captions, and boldfaced words.
Preview "The Pyramids of Giza," pages 13–14. (STOP)
Write a goal-setting question in the chart below.

Now read pages 13–14. (STOP)
Complete that section of the chart below.

Preview "The Pyramid Complex," page 15. (STOP)
Write a goal-setting question in the chart.

Read page 15. (STOP)
Complete that section of the chart.

VOCABULARY
Watch for the words you are
learning about.

immovable: not able to be moved
or relocated

leadership: guidance or direction

tombs: burial places

consumed: used up or ate

confining: tight and limiting

movable: able to be moved

confined: tight and limited

FLUENCY
Reread sentences that you find
difficult. Change your expression as
you read. Pretend you are talking to
a friend.

The Pyramids of Giza	*The Pyramid Complex*
Goal-setting question	Goal-setting question
Was my question answered, or did I have to revise it? Explain.	Was my question answered, or did I have to revise it? Explain.

AFTER YOU READ

Did you ever build a "colossal construction"? What was it?

Make Words Yours!

Learn the WORDS

As you read more about pyramids, you'll come across these words. Get to know them better.

WORD AND EXPLANATION	EXAMPLE	WRITE AN EXAMPLE
An **ideal** is a worthy idea or goal. It is a value that someone believes in.	Honesty is an important **ideal**.	What is an **ideal** that you believe in?
To be **involved** means to take part in or have a role in something.	The whole school got **involved** in the food drive.	What team or project have you been **involved** in recently?
Luxuries are unnecessary items that provide great comfort but are not affordable for most people.	Expensive sports cars and big screen TVs are **luxuries**.	What are some **luxuries** you would enjoy having?
A **passage** is a hallway or path that goes through an enclosed area.	The secret **passages** in the old house all led to a hidden room.	What would you do if you found a secret **passage**?
To **possess** something is to have it or to own it. A **possession** is an object someone owns.	You can **possess** a bicycle or a backpack.	What talents do you **possess**?
A **profession** is a job or career that requires special training or education.	Doctors and nurses are part of the medical **profession**.	What **profession** do you think you would enjoy?
If you are **reluctant**, you are unwilling to do something. **Reluctant** is the opposite of *eager*.	A dog is usually **reluctant** to give up a bone.	Why might someone be **reluctant** to go swimming?
To **resemble** means to look like something or someone else.	I almost took your book because it **resembles** mine.	What are two things in the room that **resemble** each other?

➤ YOUR TURN

In other words

Write the word from the box that means the same thing as the underlined word or phrase.

1. The rock formations <u>look like</u> a giant camel. _____

2. She believes that trust is an important <u>value</u>. _____

3. The <u>hallway</u> in the castle was cold and dark. _____

4. The little boy was <u>not eager</u> to let the nurse give him a shot. _____

5. I would give all I <u>have</u> for a chance to travel in space. _____

6. We were <u>a part of</u> the parade. _____

7. Swimming pools and diamond jewelry are <u>expensive things I don't need</u>. _____

8. Teaching is a <u>career</u> I would enjoy. _____

Choose the right word

professions   passages   ideals   luxuries

Write the word from the box that is described by each group of words or phrases.

9. doctor, engineer, lawyer

10. hall, pathway, tunnel

11. justice, fairness, honesty

12. private plane, diamond ring, big house with a pool

You've been reading about pyramids. Now show that you know the words by writing something about them.

Show that you know

Write a sentence for each word.

13. *resemble*

14. *possess*

15. *involve*

16. *reluctant*

READ on your OWN
Colossal Constructions, pages 16–19

BEFORE YOU READ

Think about the last pages you read in "The Power of Pyramids."
Who were the three pyramids of Giza built for?

AS YOU READ

To preview, look at headings, pictures, captions, and boldfaced words.
Preview "How Did They Build That?" pages 16–17. (STOP)
Write your goal-setting question in the chart below.

Now read pages 16–17. (STOP)
Complete that section of the chart below.

Preview "Masterful Building Methods," pages 18–19. (STOP)
Write your goal-setting question in the chart.

Now read pages 18–19. (STOP)
Complete that section of the chart.

How Did They Build That?	*Masterful Building Methods*
Goal-setting question	Goal-setting question
Was my question answered, or did I have to revise it? Explain.	Was my question answered, or did I have to revise it? Explain.

AFTER YOU READ

Choose one of the sections you just read. What is the most remarkable fact you learned?

ASK QUESTIONS: Question Words

Kinds of Questions

Goal-Setting	Question Words	Between the Lines	Beyond the Text
Ask, *What is my reason for reading this text?*	Ask, *What important details can I find in the text?*	Ask, *What decisions can I make about the facts and details in the text?*	Ask, *What connections can I make between the text and my life?*

Learn the STRATEGY

Asking yourself questions about the details in what you're reading will help you to remember and understand what you read. Use "question words" such as *Who? What? When? Where? Why?* or *How?* to ask questions about details. The answers to these questions can usually be found right in the text.

If you're reading about a person or people, ask a *"Who?"* question. Asking a *"What?"* question can help you remember and understand something important that happened. If you're reading about when or where an event took place, ask yourself *"When?"* or *"Where?"* questions. Asking *"Why?"* and *"How?"* questions will help you understand why events happened and how they came about.

As you read the passage below, keep asking, *Who? What? When? Where? Why? How?*

The world's tallest pyramid, the Great Pyramid, was built for King Khufu. Workers who searched the pyramid found that robbers had not broken into the pyramid and stolen the treasures. Huge blocks of rock still sealed the tunnels. Since then, experts have searched every room and passage they can find looking for the king's mummy.

So where was Khufu's mummy? It still hasn't been found. The treasures that were buried with him remain undiscovered, too. If Khufu is still in the Great Pyramid, he is in a very clever hiding place!

Below are questions that some students asked themselves as they read the passage. Circle the letters for the three questions that are answered by details in the passage. Underline the answers in the passage.

a. Why was the Great Pyramid built?
b. When did robbers break into the pyramid?
c. How did workers know that robbers had not broken in?
d. Where did the experts search for the mummy?
e. Who stole King Khufu's mummy?

YOUR TURN

Read question 1 below. Then, read "Housing an Army of Workers." Follow the directions for the other questions.

HOUSING AN
ARMY OF WORKERS

1. In this paragraph, the writer asks three questions. These questions tell you what information you will probably learn from the passage.

Circle each question.

2. Underline the answers to the three questions.

3. Look back at the answers you underlined for question 2. What did you learn about the workers who built the pyramids? Was their life easy or hard? Explain.

Thousands of workers cut, moved, and stacked the huge stone blocks of the pyramids. Where did they stay? How did they live? What kinds of things did they use or **possess**? In 1999, some of those questions were answered. That is when archaeologists discovered the workers' village at Giza.

The village is an area south of the Sphinx. Experts **involved** in the discovery believe the village was home to several thousand people at a time. Those people left behind clues about their life. Bits of grain, pieces of pottery, ash from fires, and piles of animal bones cover the area. These clues show that meals of beef, fish, and bread were cooked and served to workers in the crowded village.

The village also includes a sleeping area. There are no fancy buildings with secret **passages** here. Workers slept in mud ramps! The ramps are long trenches where 2,000 people could lie side by side. The sleeping ramps were covered by a partial roof. There were no walls and no privacy. It is easy to see that pyramid workers had a crowded home with no **luxuries** and few comforts!

Be careful to read every word so the text will make sense. Make sure you do not skip words.

FLUENCY

READ on your OWN
Colossal Constructions, pages 20–22

BEFORE YOU READ

Think about the last pages you read in "The Power of Pyramids."
How did the ancient Egyptians move the giant stone blocks?

AS YOU READ

Think about "question word" questions that ask *Who? What? When?
Where? Why?* and *How?* as you read. Place stick-on notes next to the
answers. For each section, write one of your "question word" questions,
and answer it in the chart below.

Read "A Long Way From Egypt," page 20. (STOP)

Fill in that part of the chart below. Reread the page if you need to.

Read "The Pyramids of Teotihuacán," pages 21–22. (STOP)

Fill in that part of the chart below.

VOCABULARY
Watch for the words you are learning about.

resemble: to look like something or someone

passageways: hallways or paths through enclosed areas

luxuries: items that provide great comfort and that are not affordable for most people

involved: took part in or played a role in

FLUENCY
Be careful to read every word without skipping or substituting words. If a sentence or paragraph doesn't make sense, reread every word.

A Long Way From Egypt	The Pyramids of Teotihuacán
"Question word" question	"Question word" question
Answer	Answer

AFTER YOU READ

Which would you rather visit: the Great Pyramid or the Pyramid of the Sun? Why?

Get Wordwise!
The Suffixes -ive and -ment

Learn More About the WORDS

A **suffix** is a word ending. Adding a suffix changes a word's meaning and the way it is used. The suffix **-ive** means "tending toward an action." It changes a verb to an adjective.

   Verb: Tim acts.   **Adjective:** Tim is act<u>ive</u>.

The suffix **-ment** means "state of being." It changes a verb to a noun.

   Verb: You amaze me.   **Noun:** I feel amaze<u>ment</u>.

A base word is the word before a suffix is added.

BASE WORD AND EXPLANATION	ADD -ive TO BASE WORD	WRITE AN EXAMPLE
To **protect** something means to guard or defend it against harm. Parents want to **protect** their children.	The mother cat was very _____ of her kittens.	Who is someone you are **protective** of?
To **destroy** something is to ruin it. When you add -ive to **destroy**, the new word is **destructive**.	The earthquake was _____ to homes throughout the countryside.	What else can be **destructive**?
To **possess** something means to have or own it. You can **possess** things like CDs and tennis shoes.	Some people are very _____ about their things.	How do **possessive** people act about their possessions?

WORD AND EXPLANATION	ADD -ment TO BASE WORD	WRITE AN EXAMPLE
To **enjoy** means to get great pleasure from something. We can **enjoy** watching a movie or being with someone.	Many people take pictures for _____.	What kinds of things give you **enjoyment**?
To **confine** means to keep something or someone in limits. You can **confine** your dog to the house during a storm.	The prisoner spent 10 years in _____.	Why are people with certain diseases kept in **confinement**?
To **involve** means to include or require something. Making things **involves** many steps.	Karena had a lot of _____ in the project.	Describe your **involvement** in a school activity.

Add a suffix

Complete each sentence by adding *-ive* or *-ment* to the word in parentheses.

1. **(protect)** Ancient peoples were usually _____ of their kings.

2. **(involve)** Unfortunately, Pedro's _____ in the project was minimal.

3. **(destroy)** The desert winds can be _____ to ancient buildings.

4. **(enjoy)** I always get a lot of _____ watching our football team win.

5. **(possess)** The kings of Egypt were very _____ of the treasures they had collected.

6. **(confine)** I usually like to read in the _____ of my small room.

Choose the best word

Circle the form of the word that fits the meaning of the sentence.

7. Blowing sand is the most **destroy / destructive** part of a desert storm.

8. Pyramid builders used huge boulders as **protect / protective** objects in passages.

9. Most museums **possess / possessive** valuable treasures.

10. Archaeologists must certainly find **enjoy / enjoyment** in discovering new treasures.

11. Long **confine / confinement** in the small and dusty passages must be uncomfortable.

12. Any **involve / involvement** in the discovery of a mummy must be thrilling.

Show that you know about words with suffixes. Use them to write about pyramids.

Show that you know

Write two sentences. Use at least two words from the box.

| enjoyment confinement |
| possessive destructive |

13. _____

_____

14. _____

_____

READ on your OWN
Colossal Constructions, pages 23–25

BEFORE YOU READ

Think about the last pages you read in "The Power of Pyramids." How did the Mesoamerican pyramids look like Egyptian pyramids? How did they look different?

AS YOU READ

Think about "question word" questions that ask *Who? What? When? Where? Why?* and *How?* as you read. Place stick-on notes next to the answers. For each section, write one of your "question word" questions, and answer it in the chart below.

Read "Maya Pyramids," pages 23–24. (STOP)

Fill in that part of the chart below. Reread the page if you need to.

Read "Aztec Pyramids," page 25. (STOP)

Fill in that part of the chart below.

VOCABULARY
Watch for the words you are learning about.

profession: a career that requires special education and training

reluctant: not eager

professionals: people who work in jobs that require special training and education

FLUENCY
Divide longer sentences into phrases. Read each phrase as a short sentence. Then reread the sentence.

Maya Pyramids	Aztec Pyramids
"Question word" question	"Question word" question
Answer	Answer

AFTER YOU READ

Choose the section you found most interesting. What one new fact did you learn that you would like to share?

ASK QUESTIONS: Checking Up

Kinds of Questions

Goal-Setting	**Question Words**	**Between the Lines**	**Beyond the Text**
Ask, *What is my reason for reading this text?*	Ask, *What important details can I find in the text?*	Ask, *What decisions can I make about the facts and details in the text?*	Ask, *What connections can I make between the text and my life?*

Learn the STRATEGY

Good readers stop after a paragraph or page and ask, *Did I understand what I read?* If they aren't understanding what they have read, they go back and reread the words. As they reread, they ask "question word" questions that begin with *Who? What? When? Where? Why?* or *How?*

What should you do if you're reading or rereading text and you think of a question to ask yourself? Grab a pencil. Jot your question down on an index card or a stick-on note. When you find the answer, underline it or move the stick-on note to the place where the answer appears. Doing this will help you remember important details.

Try this out as you read the passage below. On the lines to the right, jot down three questions about *Who? What? When? Where? Why?* or *How?*

About 1500 years ago, Toltec leaders in the city of Teotihuacán needed a way to keep track of the farming seasons. They watched the sun cross the sky and measured its movements. Based on their findings, they decided to make a calendar for farming.

The calendar covered 365 days. Everyone, including the city leaders, was pleased with this invention. However, as years passed, the people of Teotihuacán discovered that their calendar no longer worked! The concept of leap year had not occurred to the leaders.

Write three questions as you read. Use the "question words" provided.

1. Who _____

_____

_____

2. What _____

_____

_____

3. Why _____

_____

_____

Underline the answers you found in the text.

►YOUR TURN

Read "The Dreamers." As you read, jot down four questions about the important details in the text. Use the "question words" provided. Then write the answers to the questions. Reread if you need to in order to answer your questions.

1. Question: *Where*

Answer:

2. Question: *What*

Answer:

3. Question: *How*

Answer:

4. Question: *Why*

Answer:

THE DREAMERS

Maxtla and Tizoc were best friends. They **resembled** each other so much that they could have been brothers. Both had piercing dark eyes, jet-black hair, and high cheekbones. Like all young men their age, they enjoyed harvesting cotton, peppers, beans, and corn on their family farms in the city of Teotihuacán. Yet both men were **reluctant** to choose farming as their life's work.

One night, they sat under the stars and talked about their dreams for the future. Tizoc told his friend that he wanted to bring great honor to the **profession** of warrior. He wanted to protect his city and its people. Maxtla, however, dreamed of designing great cities and monuments, like his uncle, the builder.

The next day, Maxtla rushed to Tizoc's farm. "My uncle has arranged for us to work at the Pyramid of the Sun! Your job will be to protect the workers by chasing away wild animals, while I will chip stones. This is **ideal** training for both of us. Our new jobs will help us achieve our goals!"

Tizoc frowned. "Keeping coyotes and wolves away? Chipping at stones? How will that help us reach our goals?"

"Well," said Maxtla, "by chasing away the wild animals, you are protecting the city and our people. The pyramid will be a great monument—and I will have helped to build it. Our dreams have come true!"

Tizoc laughed and clapped his friend on the shoulder. "So they have, Maxtla."

Watch for quotation marks. Read the quoted words as the speaker would say them.

FLUENCY

READ on your OWN
Colossal Constructions, pages 26–28

BEFORE YOU READ

Think about the last pages you read in "The Power of Pyramids." Why did the Maya and Aztecs perform sacrifices?

AS YOU READ

Think about "question word" questions that ask *Who? What? When? Where? Why?* and *How?* as you read.

Choose one question that helps you remember and understand an important detail on each page of this section. Write a question for each page and enter your answer in the chart below.

VOCABULARY
Watch for the words you are learning about.

resembled: looked like something else

ideal: a high principle or value of someone's belief system

FLUENCY
Read in a smooth, relaxed manner, as if you were talking to someone. Pause after commas or periods.

Page 26	Page 27	Page 28
Question	Question	Question
Answer	Answer	Answer

AFTER YOU READ

If you were painting a ziggurat, what colors would you choose?

↓ ASK QUESTIONS: Between the Lines

Kinds of Questions

Goal-Setting	Question Words	Between the Lines	Beyond the Text
Ask, *What is my reason for reading this text?*	Ask, *What important details can I find in the text?*	Ask, *What decisions can I make about the facts and details in the text?*	Ask, *What connections can I make between the text and my life?*

Learn the STRATEGY

Some of the questions you ask as you read are answered right in the text. To answer some other questions that you ask as you read, you have to think more deeply about the text. You have to make some decisions about what the author means—but didn't come right out and say. This form of asking questions is sometimes called "reading between the lines." Here are some questions that can be answered by "reading between the lines":

Why is the author providing this information?
Why did the author choose to use these words to describe something?
What information can I find in the illustrations, captions, or graphics such as maps or timelines?
What information can I find in other parts of the text?
How does what I've read connect to what I already know?

Look at what the characters say and at the information you can find in the illustration. Then answer the questions.

Is Joe really hungry for his dinner?

_____

_____

Why might Joe have a hard time telling his mother he isn't hungry? _____

_____

_____

_____

Read "Amenemhet's Tomb." Think about the words that the author chooses to use and the information you can find in the photograph and caption. Then answer the "between the lines" questions below.

SOCIAL STUDIES CONNECTION

Amenemhet's Tomb

Amenemhet III lived in Egypt in the nineteenth century BCE. Under his rule, Egyptians lived well. Amenemhet was **involved** in improving waterways and farming for his people. However, he is best remembered for his incredible maze.

By Amenemhet's time, tomb robbing was a serious problem. Most royal tombs had been broken into, and their treasures had been stolen. Without their **luxuries**, dead pharaohs would suffer in the afterlife. Amenemhet wanted to **possess** riches after his death, so he made his pyramid into a maze to outsmart robbers.

The entrance to Amenemhet's maze was a hidden staircase on one side of the pyramid. The stairway led to a small room. The only way out was a hidden trapdoor in the ceiling. Any robber who found the exit was faced with one trick after another. Some **passages** seemed to go nowhere but actually had hidden sliding doors. At the end of the maze was Amenemhet's final trick. He was buried in a space carved in a huge block of stone. To get inside, a robber would have to lift tons of rock that were placed over the tomb.

Did Amenemhet's planning work? His burial space was finally entered in 1889. The explorers found only an empty tomb.

Amenemhet III

1. In the passage, the author never states plainly that Amenemhet III was a pharaoh of Egypt. What information tells you this fact?

2. What did the author mean by saying, "The explorers found only an empty tomb"? What does this tell you about whether or not Amenemhet's planning worked?

Change the expression in your voice to show whether information is surprising, serious, or descriptive.

FLUENCY

READ on your OWN
Colossal Constructions, pages 29–31

BEFORE YOU READ

Think about the last pages you read in "The Power of Pyramids."
Why did the Mesopotamians build ziggurats?

AS YOU READ

As you read "Pyramids of Kush," think about what the author is saying
and the words the author uses. Ask yourself questions such as *Why is the
author providing this information? Why did the author choose to use
these words to describe something?*

After you read, look at the "between the lines" questions below.
Use clues from what you read to answer. [STOP]

VOCABULARY
Watch for the words you are
learning about.

involved: took part in

ideals: high principles or values of
someone's belief system

possessions: what someone owns

professionals: people who work in
jobs that require special training
and education

resembled: looked like something
else

FLUENCY
Change your tone of voice to
emphasize points that are
interesting or amusing.

Pyramids of Kush	
"Between the lines" question Why were kings and queens removed from other burial places and taken to el-Kurru?	**Answer**
"Between the lines" question Why does the author want us to know about pyramids and ancient cultures?	**Answer**

AFTER YOU READ

Think about the chapter you just read. What is the most interesting fact you learned about Kushites?

Make Words Yours!

Learn the WORDS

Here are some words you will be reading in the next week. They are also words you need to know for your everyday reading.

WORD AND EXPLANATION	EXAMPLE	WRITE AN EXAMPLE
To **consist** of means to be made up of. A day **consists** of hours.	Our alphabet **consists** of 26 letters.	What does your favorite lunch **consist** of?
Essential describes something that is necessary. If you truly need something, it is **essential**.	Vitamins and minerals are **essential** to good health.	What is **essential** for playing a basketball game?
Something **meaningful** is important and significant.	She put a lot of thought into getting me such a **meaningful** gift.	What is something **meaningful** that you do?
When you **modify** something, you make small changes to make it better.	The band **modified** their concert schedule to add a show in Chicago.	What are ways you can **modify** your bedroom?
Something **portable** can be moved or carried.	Our smallest television is **portable**,	What can you do to make a heavy object **portable**?
Prominent describes a person or a thing that stands out because it is very noticeable or important.	Martin Luther King Jr. is a **prominent** person in American history.	What is the most **prominent** feature of the area where you live?
To **resolve** is to find an answer to a problem. It can also mean to decide to do something.	After I failed the test, I **resolved** to study harder.	What would you tell two friends to **resolve** a problem between them?
When you **restrict**, you keep something within limits. **Restrict** means the same as *confine*.	If you're on a diet, you **restrict** the amount of food you eat.	What are things some parents **restrict** their children from doing?

→YOUR TURN

Which word works?

Choose the word that fits each context and be ready to explain your choice.

1. You have a disagreement with a friend. Do you need to *modify* it or *resolve* it?
   _____

2. Without water, a person will die. Is water *prominent* or *essential*?
   _____

3. I have a small cooker I can carry on a hike. Is the cooker *meaningful* or *portable*?
   _____

4. You see a young boy playing with matches. Do you *restrict* or *consist* him from playing with matches? _____

Now show that you know the words by using them to write about buildings.

Use your own ideas

Complete each sentence in a way that makes sense.

5. The thing I would most like to *modify* is _____.

6. In my opinion, we need laws to *restrict* _____.

7. An invention I think is very useful is a *portable* _____.

8. Something that is *essential* to my happiness is _____.

9. A *meaningful* way to show a friend you care is _____.

10. My weekend *consisted* of _____.

11. A *prominent* person in my community is _____.

12. The best way to *resolve* a disagreement is by _____.

Show that you know

| consist | meaningful |
| modify | prominent |

Write four sentences. In each, use one of the words from the box.

13. _____

14. _____

15. _____

16. _____

READ on your OWN
Colossal Constructions, pages 32–35

BEFORE YOU READ

Think about what you know about skyscrapers. Why do you think people build tall structures?

AS YOU READ

As you read "Super Tall" and "Reaching for the Sky," ask yourself questions such as *What does the author want me to know about this topic?*

After you read, look at the "between the lines" questions below. Use clues from what you read to answer.

Read "Super Tall," pages 32–33. (STOP)
Fill in that part of the chart below.

Read "Reaching for the Sky," page 35. (STOP)
Fill in that part of the chart below.

VOCABULARY
Watch for the words you are learning about.

prominently: noticeably

meaningful: having a purpose

prominent: describes someone who stands out or is well known

portable: capable of being carried

resolve: determination

FLUENCY
Use your voice to emphasize any words in boldfaced type.

Super Tall	*Reaching for the Sky*
"Between the lines" question Why are tall buildings a symbol of power?	**"Between the lines" question** Why didn't Chicago build skyscrapers in their city before the Great Chicago fire?
Answer	Answer

AFTER YOU READ

Have you ever been to the top of a skyscraper? How did you feel?

↓ASK QUESTIONS: Put It Together

Kinds of Questions

Goal-Setting
Ask, *What is my reason for reading this text?*

Question Words
Ask, *What important details can I find in the text?*

Between the Lines
Ask, *What decisions can I make about the facts and details in the text?*

Beyond the Text
Ask, *What connections can I make between the text and my life?*

Learn the STRATEGY

Good readers ask themselves "between the lines" questions to help them understand what they read. To answer these questions, they must think more deeply about the text. "Thinking deeply" means making some decisions about exactly what the author means.

How do you decide on a good "between the lines" question to ask? You can try putting together information that is found in different places in the text. Think about why the author chose to include that information, and what he or she is trying to say. You can also think about why the author chose certain words to describe something in the text.

It's hard to imagine modern skyscrapers without elevators. However, when the first elevator was invented, it was very different from elevators today. It was called the Flying Chair. The device was created for the king of France in 1743. The chair was attached to a system of ropes, weights, and pulleys in the palace chimney. The king entered the chair from his balcony, and workers in the chimney slowly released the ropes. They lowered the chair down the outside of the palace. To raise the king back up, they pulled on the ropes. It made things easy for the king, but it wasn't easy for those workers who used the ropes to make the king seem to fly in his chair. They never dreamed that one day, a simple push of a button would send people "flying" to the top of tall buildings on their own!

Look at the "between the lines" questions below. Circle the letter for the information in the text that can answer the question.

Why was the first elevator called the Flying Chair?

a. It was created for the king of France in 1743.
b. Workers lowered the chair down the outside of the palace.
c. Workers used ropes to make the king seem to fly in his chair.

What did the author mean by saying that one day, "a simple push of a button would send people 'flying' to the top of tall buildings on their own"?

a. The author was talking about airplanes.
b. The author was talking about elevators in modern skyscrapers.
c. The author was talking about ropes and pulleys.

**Read "Getting to the Top."
Then answer the questions.**

GETTING TO THE TOP

1. Look at the passage. Underline the different details and pieces of information that tell you the name of the bearded inventor. Write a "between the lines" question that asks about the identity of this inventor. Then, write the answer to your question.
Question:

Answer:

2. Look at the passage. Underline the different details and pieces of information that will tell you about what elevators were like before the elevator brake was invented. Write a "between the lines" question about those first elevators. Then, write the answer to your question.
Question:

Answer:

A crowd watches nervously as a bearded man steps into an elevator on the stage. The elevator shaft is open on one side so the audience can see what happens inside. A rope carries the elevator halfway up the shaft. Then the bearded man gives his partner a **meaningful** nod. The partner chops the rope in two. The audience gasps!

The elevator didn't fall when the rope broke that day in 1854. Why didn't it fall? A device invented by that bearded man locked the elevator in place. For many years, the device was a **prominent** feature on most elevators.

Though this inventor didn't invent the elevator, he made it better. His special brake was **essential** for elevators in tall buildings. Before that time, architects didn't dream of designing buildings over four stories tall. It would have been too risky for people to travel higher than that in an elevator.

With an elevator that couldn't fall, architects didn't have to **restrict** the height of buildings. Before long, city skylines shot towards the sky. The bearded inventor had helped usher in the age of skyscrapers. Today, Elisha Otis's name lives on in the Otis Elevator Company.

Show expression in your voice by letting it rise at the end of a question when reading.

FLUENCY

READ on your OWN
Colossal Constructions, pages 36–38

BEFORE YOU READ

Think about the last pages you read in "Superscrapers." Why was there a lot of construction in Chicago in the late nineteenth century?

AS YOU READ

As you read "From Stone to Steel," think about how you can use the information or the author's words to come up with a good "between the lines" question.

After you read this section, write a "between the lines" question that compares skyscrapers built of stone to skyscrapers built of steel. Then, write the answer. Use the first set of boxes below. (STOP)

Now write a "between the lines" question about the words "bones in the human body." Think about the author's reason for using these words to talk about a skyscraper. After you write the question, then write the answer. Use the second set of boxes below. (STOP)

From Stone to Steel

"Between the lines" question	Answer
"Between the lines" question	Answer

AFTER YOU READ

Choose a fact from this section that you would like to share with someone else.

Get Wordwise!
Words With Latin Roots

Learn More About the WORDS

Many of the words we use today were borrowed from the ancient language of **Latin**. A **root** is the most basic word part. Learning the meaning of roots that come from Latin can help you figure out the meaning of many unfamiliar words.

The definitions below connect the meaning of Latin roots to the meaning of some English words. Use the meaning of the Latin roots to complete the definitions.

ROOT	LATIN MEANING	RELATED WORDS & MEANING	WRITE ANSWERS
port	carry	**transport:** to _____ from one place to another	What is something you *transport* to and from school?
		export: to _____ goods out of one country to another	What would you *export* if you had your own business?
sist	stand	**resist:** to _____ up against something	Why might someone *resist* your offer for help?
		assist: to take a _____ to help	When might you need someone to *assist* you?
solve	loosen or release	**solve:** to _____ the answer locked in a problem	What kinds of puzzles do you like to *solve*?
		dissolve: to _____ up and become part of a liquid	When does sugar *dissolve*?
strict	tight	**strict:** keeping _____ control over others	Why might a parent be *strict* with a child?
		constrict: to make _____	When might you feel *constricted*?

YOUR TURN

Match words and meanings

Use what you know about Latin roots to match each word to its meaning. You can use the chart on page 91 for help.

chart on page 91 for help.

```
assist   export   dissolve   constrict
```

1. To loosen up and become part of a liquid: _____

2. To make narrow or tight: _____

3. To carry goods out of a country: _____

4. To take a stand to support something: _____

Modify the paragraph

```
resist   transport   solve   strict
```

5. **Cross out four words or phrases in the paragraph that can be replaced with the words from the box.**

6. **Above each word you cross out, write the replacement word. Read the modified paragraph to be sure it makes sense.**

Now use the words with Latin roots to write something about skyscrapers.

Eddie and Cristina thought their parents were too controlling. Their parents thought the kids were too young to drive to places on their own. Eventually, they found a way to answer the problem. Eddie and Cristina promised not to stand up against their parents' offer to drive them to evening activities.

Show that you know

Write four sentences. Use at least one word from each pair of words in the box.

```
assist/resist      export/transport
solve/dissolve     strict/constrict
```

7. _____

8. _____

9. _____

10. _____

READ on your OWN
Colossal Constructions, pages 39–41

BEFORE YOU READ

Think about the last pages you read in "Superscrapers." How is the steel skeleton of a building like a human skeleton? How are the outside walls like curtains?

AS YOU READ

As you read "Dueling Skyscrapers" and "Higher," think about how you can use the information or the author's words to come up with a good "between the lines" question.

Read "Dueling Skyscrapers," page 39. (STOP)
Write a "between the lines" question that compares the architects Craig Severance and William Van Alen.

Read "Higher," pages 40–41. (STOP)
Write a "between the lines" question about the author's use of the words "like a needle in his heart."

Dueling Skyscrapers	Higher
"Between the lines" question	"Between the lines" question
Answer	Answer

AFTER YOU READ

Do you think the "race" between Severance and Van Alen was an important one? Why or why not?

↓ ASK QUESTIONS: What You Already Know

Kinds of Questions

Goal-Setting	Question Words	Between the Lines	Beyond the Text
Ask, *What is my reason for reading this text?*	Ask, *What important details can I find in the text?*	Ask, *What decisions can I make about the facts and details in the text?*	Ask, *What connections can I make between the text and my life?*

Learn the STRATEGY

You have already learned that good readers ask "between the lines" questions in order to understand what they read. To ask some of these questions, you put information in the text together with other information that is there.

There is another kind of "between the lines" question to ask. To come up with this type of question, you first think about what information is stated directly in the text. Next, you think about how that information fits together with what you already know about the people or events in the text.

Read the passage. Think about what you already know about the people or events in the text.

Did you know that a special group of people has worked on every major building project in New York City since the 1920s? Native American ironworkers from the Mohawk nation have helped to build many important buildings in New York, including the Empire State Building and Madison Square Garden.

The tradition started in 1886, when a railway company built a bridge on Mohawk land between Canada and New York State. The company hired Mohawks to work on the bridge. The workers were so skilled at working at great heights that they were nicknamed "skywalkers." As the New York skyline began to stretch upward, many Mohawk ironworkers moved to the New York City area.

Write a sentence about what you already know about the buildings that make up New York City's skyline.

_____

_____

Put the information you already know about New York City's skyline together with what the text tells you about Mohawk ironworkers. Then answer the "between the lines" question.

Question: Why did Mohawk ironworkers move to New York City as the skyline began to stretch upward?

Answer: _____

_____

_____

_____

►YOUR TURN

As you read "Lonely at the Top," think about what you already know about the characters and events in the passage. Use what you know to ask questions about the main character's thoughts, feelings, and actions.

Lonely AT THE TOP

1. After reading the title and the first paragraph, what questions do you have?

2. This paragraph gives clues about Katsi's problem. What does it make you wonder?

3. Read between the lines. What do you think Katsi will do?

As the New York afternoon grew warmer, Katsi's welding equipment seemed to grow heavier. She couldn't get her mind off her problem. She could see both sides of the issue, but she couldn't **resolve** it. Such distractions could be deadly to an ironworker working 80 stories above the ground.

"Let's break!" called the foreman. The workers took their break and moved into the shade. Katsi sat apart, listening to music on her **portable** CD player.

"My days **consist** of dangerous work, which I love," she thought gloomily, "but I should be someplace else right now." Katsi pulled a photograph of an eighteen-year-old boy from her pocket. She looked at it and smiled. As a child, her son Rex had loved skyscraper stories. She had told him many times about his great-grandfather's work on the Empire State Building. Like many Mohawks, Katsi's grandfather and uncles had been ironworkers. Rex was proud of the family tradition. Today, though, was a big day for him, and Katsi wasn't there. Would he understand? *I can still get there in time*, she thought.

The break ended, but Katsi sat on, lost in thought. The foreman approached, and Katsi realized she would have to **modify** her attitude. She took off her headset and looked up at the foreman. What she saw in his understanding face helped her make her decision.

Let your expression and tone of voice reflect what the character is feeling.

FLUENCY

READ on your OWN
Colossal Constructions, pages 42–44

BEFORE YOU READ

Think about the last pages you read in "Superscrapers." Why did Van Alen add floors and a spire to his plans for the Chrysler Building?

AS YOU READ

As you read "The Eighth Wonder of the World," think about how the information you are reading fits together with what you already know about building skyscrapers. Use what you know to write a "between the lines" question for each page.

Read page 42. (STOP)
Fill in that part of the chart below.

Read page 43. (STOP)
Fill in that part of the chart below.

Read page 44. (STOP)
Fill in that part of the chart below.

Page 42	Page 43	Page 44
"Between the lines" question	"Between the lines" question	"Between the lines" question
Answer	Answer	Answer

VOCABULARY
Watch for the words you are learning about.

prominent: standing out; readily noticeable

essential: necessary

consist: to be made up of

consisting: being made up of

portable: capable of being moved

FLUENCY
Match your expression and tone of voice to the feeling of what you are reading.

AFTER YOU READ

Think about the section you just read. What is something you would like to explain to someone else?

↓ ASK QUESTIONS: Beyond the Text

Kinds of Questions

Goal-Setting
Ask, *What is my reason for reading this text?*

Question Words
Ask, *What important details can I find in the text?*

Between the Lines
Ask, *What decisions can I make about the facts and details in the text?*

Beyond the Text
Ask, *What connections can I make between the text and my life?*

Learn the STRATEGY

Only you can answer some of the questions that come to your mind as you read. Asking these kinds of questions is thinking "beyond the text." When you think beyond the text, you connect what you are reading to your own life. You relate the words to your own thoughts, feelings, and experiences.

Why do good readers ask beyond the text questions? When you connect what you read to the real world, it's easier to understand what you read.

Look at the comic strip and ask some questions that go beyond the text.

What would I do if

_____

_____

_____?

How would it feel to

_____

_____

_____?

What if _____

_____

_____?

➤ YOUR TURN

Read "Skyscraper Design." Think about what you are learning as you read and how it relates to your own thoughts, feelings, and experiences. Then, write two questions that connect what you are reading to your own life. Your questions might start with "How would I feel about...?" or "What if I...?" or "Would I like...?"

SCIENCE CONNECTION

Skyscraper Design

Designing a skyscraper is a very rewarding job. The architect gets to see a plan that he or she has created turn into a magnificent structure. However, designing a skyscraper involves much more than drawing a picture of a building. Architects and engineers must make sure that the building will be strong, safe, and practical.

An underground foundation supports a skyscraper. All the weight in the building is transferred to vertical steel columns built on this foundation. If the foundation is weak, the buildings can crack or even collapse. Great attention to detail is needed.

Safety issues must be **resolved**. There must be enough elevators and stairways for emergency use. Large windows must be strong enough to resist shattering. At the

Architects need to make sure their buildings are safe.

same time, they must be lightweight enough that the building can support them.

A skyscraper design must also fit a budget. An architect might like a large beautiful, spacious lobby. However, a large lobby could **restrict** the space left for offices. In the end, an architect has to serve the needs of his or her clients.

1. Question:

Answer:

2. Question:

Answer:

As you read and reread, pay attention to punctuation marks that are clues to correct phrasing.

FLUENCY

READ on your OWN
Colossal Constructions, pages 45–48

BEFORE YOU READ

Think about the last pages you read in "Superscrapers."
How did the Great Depression help in the construction of the
Empire State Building?

AS YOU READ

As you read "How Are Skyscrapers Designed and Built?" and
"Constructing a Skyscraper," ask beyond the text questions that relate
your reading to your thoughts, feelings, and experiences.

Read **"How Are Skyscrapers Designed and Built?" pages 45–46.** (STOP)
Fill in the chart below. The first question is given as an example.

Read **"Constructing a Skyscraper," pages 47–48.** (STOP)
Fill in that part of the chart below.

Page	Beyond the text question	Answer
45	*If a company wanted me to build a skyscraper, what shape might I choose?*	
46		
47		
48		

AFTER YOU READ

Would you rather do an architect's job or an engineer's? Why?

Make Words Yours!

Learn the WORDS

In this week's reading about skyscrapers, you'll come across these words. Read on and get to know them better.

WORD AND EXPLANATION	EXAMPLE	WRITE AN EXAMPLE
Adequate means enough. Something that is **adequate** fills a certain need.	A plant cannot live without an **adequate** supply of water.	What would be an **adequate** number of CDs for you to own?
A **foundation** is the underground base of a building. It can also mean the basis or principle upon which something stands.	The workers poured a concrete **foundation** for the house.	Why is a good education the **foundation** for a good job?
When you **internalize** something, you make it personal or part of your own thinking.	After playing the song on the piano for two weeks, I began to **internalize** the notes.	What do you do to help **internalize** the meanings of new words?
To **lessen** is to shrink in degree or number. **Lessen** is a synonym for *decrease*.	Sometimes soft music and soft lights can **lessen** stress.	What can you do to **lessen** the chance of getting injured playing a sport?
An **occupant** is a person who is in or lives in a place.	The restaurant can have a maximum of 180 **occupants**.	How many **occupants** are in your classroom?
If something is done **partially**, it isn't done completely. It isn't finished.	We were **partially** done with the baseball game when it began to rain.	What might a teacher say if your homework is **partially** finished?
Progressive means making use of new ideas or moving forward.	In colonial times, the ideas in the U.S. Constitution were very **progressive**.	If you were running for class president, what **progressive** ideas would you suggest?
When you **utilize** something you make use of it.	Dad **utilized** the lawn mower to cut grass.	What rooms of your home do you **utilize** the most?

►YOUR TURN

True or False?

Write *true* or *false* and be ready to explain your answer.

1. You can *utilize* a pencil to make dinner. _____

2. If you *partially* pay for a shirt, you have paid in full. _____

3. If you *internalize* a song, you don't know it. _____

4. To *lessen* your chances means that something is more likely to happen. _____

Choose the right word

utilize	partially	occupants	lessen
internalize	progressive	adequate	foundation

Fill each blank with a word from the box.

5. An ice pack can _____ pain.

6. The Constitution is the _____ of our system of government.

7. There are three _____ in the house next door.

8. The carpenter will _____ all of his tools to finish the job.

9. It takes a lot of _____ ideas to bring about change.

10. I didn't have _____ time to finish the job.

11. I was _____ finished with my essay, so I didn't hand it in.

12. I often _____ people's problems and try to solve them.

You've read about designing a skyscraper. Now show that you know the words by writing about it.

Show that you know

Use your own ideas to complete each sentence.

13. Buildings need to have *adequate* _____

14. To *lessen* the chance of safety problems, _____

15. The *foundation* of a skyscraper should be strong because _____

16. If a building will have many *occupants*, the design should include _____

READ on your OWN
Colossal Constructions, pages 49–51

BEFORE YOU READ

Think about the last pages you read in "Superscrapers." What professionals are involved in building a skyscraper?

AS YOU READ

Read "Superstructures," pages 49–50. (STOP)

Read "Open for Business," page 51. (STOP)

Write beyond the text questions and answers in the chart below. The first question is done as an example.

Page	Question	Answer
49	*Would I like to be a welder on a skyscraper?*	

VOCABULARY

Watch for the words you are learning about.

foundations: the underlying supports

utilized: used

partially: not completely

lessens: shrinks in degree; decreases

utilize: to use

occupants: people who fill space in a building

FLUENCY

Emphasize important phrases by the way you read them.

AFTER YOU READ

Choose a page and tell something on that page that surprised you.

↓ ASK QUESTIONS: Two Kinds of Questions

Kinds of Questions

Goal-Setting
Ask, *What is my reason for reading this text?*

Question Words
Ask, *What important details can I find in the text?*

Between the Lines
Ask, *What decisions can I make about the facts and details in the text?*

Beyond the Text
Ask, *What connections can I make between the text and my life?*

Learn the STRATEGY

You have learned that good readers ask themselves different kinds of questions as they read. "Between the lines" questions are questions that require you to think more deeply about the text. You think about the information the author has chosen to include and what he or she is trying to say. You also think about why the author chose certain words to describe people or events. To ask "beyond the text" questions, you think about what you are reading in another way. You ask questions that help you connect what you read to your thoughts, feelings, and experiences. Both of these kinds of questions will help you to understand and remember what you read.

The passage below is part of a story. After you've read it, answer the questions in the margins.

Use the question starter to ask yourself a "between the lines" question. Write the question and the answer. Then, use the question starter to ask yourself a "beyond the text" question. Write the question and the answer.

Between the lines question starter:

Why does the author use the words _____
_____
_____

Answer: _____
_____

Beyond the text question starter:

How would I feel if _____
_____
_____
_____

Answer: _____
_____

LOOKING UP

Grant Myers leaned against an iron fence and scowled. The look on his face was about as welcoming as the tall fence.

"Good morning, Myers!" said Walter Parks brightly.

"No, it isn't. Hasn't been a good morning since we finished work on that place," said Myers. He nodded toward the Empire State Building.

"It's 1932! This Depression can't keep New York City down for long," said Parks. He stood a sign that said NEED WORK on the sidewalk, then took his place beside Myers.

"Someone's going to build another skyscraper real soon," Parks said confidently. "We'll be the first people they'll turn to for workers."

→YOUR TURN

As you read "High Stakes," ask "between the lines" questions and "beyond the text" questions. Ask questions that require you to think more deeply about what you are reading, and questions that help you relate what you read to your own thoughts, feelings, and experiences.

1. *I wonder what it would be like to*

2. *What kind of rumors has Myra probably*

3. *Would I have patience to*

4. *What might be one reason why Myra*

The office was strangely quiet as Myra King worked alone late into the night. There were no other **occupants** in the office cubicles. Myra planned to stay until she finished the job. At ten o'clock the next morning, she would present her model to J. W. Pratt, the man who would build and own the skyscraper.

Myra was a model maker. She had worked for weeks to bring the architect's plan to life. First, she entered hundreds of the skyscraper's measurements into a computer program. Then, she **utilized** the program to create pictures of every piece of the building. After printing out the pictures, Myra glued them onto thick, stiff paper, cut them out, and fitted them together.

Everyone assured Myra that the model would sell the skyscraper and that the other architectural firms didn't have a chance. Kind words couldn't **lessen** the nervousness she felt. She had heard rumors about the way that J. W. Pratt treated people who didn't live up to his expectations.

At sunup, Myra was still working. The early morning light filled the office and made her **partially** completed model glow. It looked breathtaking. She thought, *If my model wins the bid for our firm, I'll really prove that I have what it takes.*

Practice reading until you can read without mistakes. Then read the passage smoothly and at a pace that seems natural.

FLUENCY

READ on your OWN
Colossal Constructions, pages 52–54

BEFORE YOU READ

Think about the last pages you read in "Superscrapers." How is building a skyscraper like putting together a model airplane?

AS YOU READ

As you read "Today's Tallest Skyscrapers," ask yourself "between the lines" questions and "beyond the text" questions. Remember, "between the lines" questions require you to think more deeply about what you are reading. "Beyond the text" questions help you relate what you read to your own thoughts, feelings, and experiences.

The Idea Web below provides "question starters" for between the lines questions on the left side of the circle. "Question starters" for beyond the text questions are on the right side.

Read page 52. (STOP)
Fill in some of the Idea Web questions.

Read page 54. (STOP)
Fill in some of the Idea Web questions.

Read page 53. (STOP)
Fill in some of the Idea Web questions.

VOCABULARY
Watch for the words you are learning about.

occupants: people who live in a building

lessen: to shrink in degree or number; to decrease

utilized: used

occupancy: the condition of living somewhere as a tenant or an owner

partially: not completely

FLUENCY
Try to read without mistakes and at an appropriate pace.

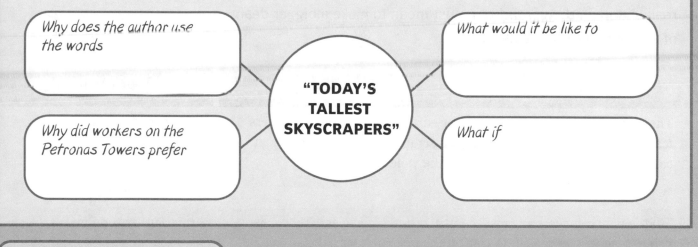

- Why does the author use the words
- Why did workers on the Petronas Towers prefer
- "TODAY'S TALLEST SKYSCRAPERS"
- What would it be like to
- What if

AFTER YOU READ

Would you want to walk over the sky bridge that connects the Petronas Towers? Why or why not?

Get Wordwise!
Context Clues

Learn More About the WORDS

Jason told everyone that he had saved a little girl's life.
However, Jason greatly **aggrandized** his part in the rescue.
It was April who pulled the little girl out of the raging water.
Jason merely handed the girl a towel.

In the paragraph, you see a long word like *aggrandized*.
You think, "What does THAT mean? I don't have a clue!" Well,
there are usually some clues right under your nose.

Words and phrases that help you figure out the meaning of a
word are called **context clues**.

To find the clues, first, you reread the sentence the word appears
in. Hmmm. *Aggrandized* could mean lots of things. You need
more. You look at the sentences before and after. Jason said he
had saved the girl's life, but what he actually did was hand her a
towel. Now we're getting somewhere. Jason exaggerated what
really happened. *Aggrandized* must mean to make a bigger deal
of something than it really is.

WORD IN CONTEXT	WRITE AN EXPLANATION
The skyscraper in Taipei is at risk for earthquake damage. Engineers fear that the safety features in the skyscraper are **inadequate**. In an earthquake, the skyscraper would shake violently.	I think **inadequate** means
That is why engineers suggest the **utilization** of dampers. They hope using them will be enough to control the building's vibrations.	I think **utilization** means

►YOUR TURN

Synonym? Yes or No?

Look for context clues in these sentences. Then decide whether the word in the box is a synonym for the underlined word.

FIND CONTEXT CLUES	SYNONYM?	YES/NO?
1. The student's preparation was <u>inadequate</u>, so he failed the test.	enough	
2. The man tried to <u>impart</u> his knowledge of ironworking to his son.	share	
3. The beginner's class provided important <u>foundational</u> information.	basic	
4. While she waited, Ana <u>occupied</u> her time by reading a magazine.	collected	

Use context clues

Underline the context clues that help you figure out the meaning of the boldfaced words. Then, write their meanings.

Ray was **preoccupied** all day by the soreness in his ankle. He worried that the ice pack and rest would not be enough to get rid of the pain. He was right. His ankle was getting **progressively** worse. Slowly and surely, he was in more pain by the time he got to the stadium.

The coach took one look at him and said, "Tough break, Ray. I know how much you wanted to quarterback this game. Tyrone has trained **adequately** though, and he'll do a good job in your place."

Ray pictured Tyrone **occupying** his place on the field. When he thought about someone else filling his space as quarterback, Ray fought back tears of disappointment.

EXPLANATION
5. preoccupied:
6. progressively:
7. adequately:
8. occupying:

You've read about skyscrapers. Now use the words to write about them.

Show that you know

Write a sentence for each word.

9. *progressively*

10. *utilization*

READ on your OWN
Colossal Constructions, pages 55–57

BEFORE YOU READ

Think about the last pages you read in "Superscrapers." What buildings have been the world's tallest since the Sears Tower lost the title?

AS YOU READ

As you read page 55 of "9/11 and Beyond" and pages 56–57 of "Emotions Run High," ask yourself "between the lines" and "beyond the text" questions. (STOP)

Record your questions on the list below. The question starters may give you some ideas.

VOCABULARY
Watch for the words you are learning about.

internalize: to take in values

progressed: moved forward

foundations: the underlying supports

progressive: moving upward

FLUENCY
Pay attention to punctuation. Punctuation marks can tell you when to pause and when to raise your voice for a question or an exclamation.

Pages 55–57
Why are there so many emotions about
What if
How is the new Freedom Tower like
What would it be like to
Could I

AFTER YOU READ

Choose a section you just read. What is something you will explain to someone else?

ASK QUESTIONS: All Kinds of Questions

Kinds of Questions

Goal-Setting
Ask, *What is my reason for reading this text?*

Question Words
Ask, *What important details can I find in the text?*

Between the Lines
Ask, *What decisions can I make about the facts and details in the text?*

Beyond the Text
Ask, *What connections can I make between the text and my life?*

Learn the STRATEGY

You've learned to ask different kinds of questions to help you understand and remember what you read. When you finish reading a paragraph or a page, ask yourself a very important question: *Did I understand what I read?*

If you didn't understand, go back and reread the words. As you read again, ask yourself questions. You can ask goal-setting questions, which help to give you a reason for reading. You can ask "question word" questions that begin with *Who? What? When? Where? Why?* or *How?* You can also ask "between the lines" questions, where you put together the facts and details in the text to make decisions about it. Finally, you can ask "beyond the text" questions, which help you make connections between what you read and your own life.

NOWHERE TO GO BUT UP!

Extreme climbers use special equipment to climb some of the tallest skyscrapers in the world. However, only the man they call Spiderman climbs tall buildings with his bare hands and feet. He doesn't even use a safety net!

Spiderman's real name is Alain Robert. He has climbed 70 skyscrapers, including the Sears and Petronas Towers, as an unusual hobby.

It's amazing that Robert is able to climb at all. He was injured in rock-climbing accidents before he began climbing skyscrapers. Doctors said he would never climb again.

Ask and answer the different kinds of questions you've learned about.

Goal-setting question:
_____
_____

Answer: _____
_____

"Question word" question:
_____
_____

Answer: _____
_____

"Between the lines" question:
_____
_____

Answer: _____
_____

"Beyond the text" question:
_____
_____

Answer: _____
_____

➤YOUR TURN

Read "Climbing the Walls." Stop at the end of each paragraph and ask yourself, *Did I understand what I read?* As you read, ask and answer the different kinds of questions that can help you understand and remember what you read.

1. Question

Answer

2. Question

Answer

3. Question

Answer

4. Question

Answer

Climbing the Walls

Wouldn't it be great to climb skyscrapers the way superheroes do? However, ordinary people don't have superhuman skills. A window washer can't climb to the eightieth floor to scrub windows. Emergency workers can't scale walls to save people trapped in a skyscraper—or can they? If they have the latest technology, they can!

Gerald Winkler's **progressive** ideas are creating a new generation of climbers. His climbing invention helps emergency workers in high-rise rescues. Climbers strap one of Winkler's special suction cups to each hand and foot. Then compressed air is piped into the cups to create a vacuum seal. When there is **adequate** suction to support a step up, lights on the suction cups let the climber know. Of course, the climbers must still **internalize** feelings of confidence in their ability to climb tall buildings. The invention doesn't help them overcome a fear of heights.

There's high-tech help for window washers, too. A German company used similar technology to create a window-washing robot. The robot can clean a skyscraper from **foundation** to top all by itself. The robot soaps, rinses, and even dries the windows. All workers do is refill the machine when the soap runs out!

Climbing inventions like this window-washing robot are used to wash windows.

Practice reading difficult sentences in a passage. Then practice until you can read the entire passage without mistakes.

FLUENCY

READ on your OWN
Colossal Constructions, **pages 58–60**

BEFORE YOU READ

Think about the last pages you read in "Superscrapers." What did the winning design for a new skyscraper at the World Trade Center site look like?

AS YOU READ

Think about the different kinds of questions you've learned to ask. Then, read "High Anxiety" and "A Look to the Future," pages 58–60. (STOP)

Write four questions, the kind of questions they are, and the answers to the questions in the chart below.

Question	Kind of question	Answer

VOCABULARY
Watch for the words you are learning about.

occupied: filled or taken up

adequate: sufficient or enough

foundations: the principles upon which something stands

foundation: underlying support

progress: a forward movement

FLUENCY
When words or sentences are difficult, practice reading them accurately until you can read them without mistakes.

AFTER YOU READ

What is one fact that surprised you on the pages you just read?

Unit 2 Reflection

VOCABULARY

The words that were newest to me were

The words I'll probably use the most are

I still need to work on

Colossal Constructions

COMPREHENSION

The kind of question that helped me the most is

The hardest part of asking questions is

I still need to work on

FLUENCY

I am reading more fluently because I worked on

I still need to work on

INDEPENDENT READING

My favorite part of Colossal Constructions is

GREAT
UNSOLVED MYSTERIES

COMPREHENSION
LEARN THE POWER OF MAKING PREDICTIONS

INDEPENDENT READING
Great Unsolved Mysteries
Includes "On Treasure's Trail" and
"Mysteries of History"

unit 3 B

VOCABULARY

WORDS:
Know them!
Use them!
Learn all about them!

FLUENCY
Make your reading
smooth and accurate,
one tip at a time.

Make Words Yours!

Learn the WORDS

Here are some words you will be reading in the next week. They are also words you need to know for your everyday reading.

WORD AND EXPLANATION	EXAMPLE	WRITE AN EXAMPLE
A **conquest** is something gained by force or great effort.	The mountain climber's **conquest** of Mount Everest was impressive.	What other types of **conquests** might someone achieve?
To **defeat** means to beat an enemy or opponent. If you **defeat** the other team, you win.	Our basketball team is strong enough to **defeat** anyone in the league.	In what sport could you **defeat** your friends?
When you **extend** something, you spread or stretch it out. You can **extend** your arms and you can **extend** a vacation.	If the shipwreck isn't found this week, the divers will **extend** their search.	When have you asked someone to **extend** a deadline?
If you **increase** something, you make it larger in number or amount.	If the diggers find any gold coins, interest in the site will **increase**.	How can you **increase** your strength?
To **insert** is to put something into something else.	Jason had to **insert** the key into the lock to open the door.	When might you **insert** a coin into something?
If you **preserve** something, you keep it safe and free from damage.	The city raised money to **preserve** the old building.	Why might someone want to **preserve** a tree?
When you **profit** from something, you gain wealth or something of value from it.	Erin hopes to **profit** from selling the crafts she made.	What skill do you have that you could **profit** from?
If you **recover**, you return to normal. If you **recover** something, you get it back.	It took Tyrone several months to **recover** his health after being sick.	When have you been able to **recover** something you lost?

➤YOUR TURN

Answer these questions and be ready to explain your answers.

1. Do you *insert* film into a camera before taking pictures? _____

2. If your favorite team *defeated* another team, would you be happy? _____

3. If a country lost a war, would you call it a *conquest*? _____

4. If you add another day to a trip, do you *extend* it? _____

Choose the right word

extend   increase   conquest   preserve
insert   profit   defeat   recover

Fill each blank with the correct word from the box.

5. Tony was able to [_____] his opponent.

6. Studying will [_____] your chances of getting an *A*.

7. The toy company will [_____] from the popular board game.

8. The king's [_____] of new land was very costly.

9. The search team tried to [_____] the missing vehicle.

10. Please [_____] the letter into the envelope.

11. Sonia put the photographs in an album to [_____] them.

12. My teacher won't [_____] the deadline for my paper.

Show that you know the words by answering questions about treasure hunting.

Show that you know

Answer the questions. Use sentences.

13. How could you *profit* from finding treasure?

14. What kind of treasure would you like to *recover*?

15. What would *increase* your chances of finding a treasure?

16. What kind of treasure would you *preserve*?

READ on your OWN
Great Unsolved Mysteries, pages 3–6

BEFORE YOU READ

Think about the title of the first chapter, "The Lure of Treasure."
What do you think might lure someone to search for treasure?

AS YOU READ

Read page 3 of "The Lure of Treasure." (STOP)
Complete the following sentence.

One thing that keeps a treasure hunter going day after day is

_____

_____ .

Read "Seeking Treasure," pages 4–5. (STOP)

Complete the following sentence.

One place a treasure hunter might begin to search for treasure is

to look for _____

_____ .

Read page 6 of "The Glow of El Dorado." (STOP)

Complete the following sentences.

"El Dorado" is Spanish for _____ .

Spanish explorers used the words "El Dorado" to refer to

_____

_____ .

AFTER YOU READ

What is the most interesting treasure you read about today? Why do you think so?

_____

VOCABULARY
Watch for the words you are learning about.

extend: to spread or stretch out

conquest: something gained by force

increase: to become larger in amount

FLUENCY
Use commas and periods as a guide for when to pause during reading.

PREDICT: Previewing

How to Predict

| **Preview text features** to get an idea of what you will be reading about. | **Use what you know** to predict what will happen next. | Use different skills to **preview fiction and nonfiction**. | **Check** your predictions. You can confirm them or change your prediction. | **Elaborate** on your predictions. |

Learn the STRATEGY

In order to understand what they are reading, good readers always preview the text features. When you preview, you give the text a very quick look to get an idea of what it is about and to help set a goal for reading. Text features such as book titles, chapter titles, and headings can all provide clues to what the text is about. These features also tell you about the way in which the material is organized. Another way to look for clues before reading is to preview the pictures or illustrations and their captions and to look at any boldfaced or italicized words.

Look at the cover of the book the girl in the illustration is holding. What two clues on the cover suggest what the book is about?

_____

_____

Based on these two clues, what do you think the book is about?

_____

_____

_____

➤YOUR TURN

Gold bars found by
Mel Fisher on a shipwreck

TREASURE HUNTER

As a boy, Mel Fisher dreamed of finding treasure from a pirate **conquest**. However, Mel lived a thousand miles from the ocean—too far away to follow his dream.

Years later Mel moved to Florida. He and his wife Dolores took up deep-sea diving. Together, they explored old shipwrecks. Then they moved to California. They opened a dive shop where they could train divers and make underwater films.

Then Mel joined a diving team. The team was searching for Spanish ships that had sunk off the coast of Florida in 1715. To assist the team, Mel invented a special tube that he called the "mailbox." The tube **extended** from the surface of the water to the bottom of the ocean. The tube carried clear water to the sandy bottom. The clear water **increased** visibility so that the divers could see what was around them. With the help of Mel's invention, the divers on his team discovered more than 1,000 gold coins.

Mel went on to find other shipwrecks. He and his team found more than 20 million dollars worth of gold and treasures from one wreck. However, Mel was not interested in riches alone. He started a museum in Key West, Florida, to **preserve** and display his treasures.

Preview "Treasure Hunter" before reading it. Follow the numbered directions.

1. Identify the clues that tell you what this passage is about.

2. Write in the space below what you think you will be reading about.

Read the passage and answer question 3.

3. Was the passage about what you predicted it would be? Explain.

Remember to pause at commas and periods as you read.

FLUENCY

READ on your OWN
Great Unsolved Mysteries, pages 7–9

BEFORE YOU READ

Think about the last pages you read in "On Treasure's Trail." Why did the Spanish explorers call the king and the land in South America "El Dorado"?

AS YOU READ

Preview all the text features in "Seekers of El Dorado" to predict what you will be reading about on pages 7–9. (STOP)
Complete the first two sentences in the chart below. Then read pages 7–9 and answer the last question.

Seekers of El Dorado

I predict this section will be about

To make my prediction, I looked at

Did your prediction help you to think about the ideas in this passage? Why or why not?

VOCABULARY
Watch for the words you are learning about.

defeat: to win

preserve: to keep something safe

extended: offered

conquest: something gained by force

FLUENCY
Watch for commas and read phrases as short sentences.

AFTER YOU READ

Choose the most interesting page and tell something you would like to share on that page.

Get Wordwise!
Antonyms

Learn More About the WORDS

Some words are opposites. Two words that mean opposite things are called **antonyms**.

Something that is **immovable** cannot be moved.

Something that is **portable** can be moved or carried.

The words *immovable* and *portable* are antonyms.

WORD AND EXPLANATION	ANTONYM AND EXPLANATION	CIRCLE THE WORD
preserve: to keep safe from harm	**destroy:** to break up or ruin	Carlos wanted to **preserve / destroy** his childhood home because he had so many happy memories of it.
increase: to become larger or to make something larger	**decrease:** to become smaller or to make something smaller	Jane was saving money to **increase / decrease** the size of her bank account.
profit: to gain wealth or something of value	**lose:** to have less or to get rid of wealth	Will wanted to **profit / lose** from his invention.
recover: to return to normal or to get something back	**lose:** to be unable to find	Melissa was grateful to the people who helped her **recover / lose** her necklace.
insert: to put something into something else	**remove:** to take something out of something else	Hana asked me to **insert / remove** the clean dishes from the dishwasher.
extend: to spread or stretch out in length or time	**shorten:** to reduce or make smaller in length or time	The tired players were happy when their coach decided to **extend / shorten** practice.
conquest: something gained by force or great effort	**loss:** something not won	The soldiers were pleased with their **conquest / loss** of the enemy forces.

➡ YOUR TURN

Write the antonym

conquest   portable   extend   increase
insert   preserve   profit   recover

Write a word from the box that means the opposite of the word in parentheses.

1. **(loss)** The climbers stood at the top and celebrated their _____ of the mountain.

2. **(remove)** You need to _____ batteries into the radio to make it work.

3. **(lose)** Do you think you will _____ from the garage sale?

4. **(destroy)** We recycle to help _____ the environment.

5. **(decrease)** The chance of rain will _____ by morning.

6. **(shorten)** How far can you _____ the rope?

7. **(lose)** After a long search, Ben was able to _____ his dog.

8. **(immovable)** The small television was _____ so we took it with us on our trip.

Show that you know about antonyms. Use the pairs below to write about any kind of treasure.

Show that you know

Choose two of the word pairs. Write a sentence for each word in those pairs.

preserve/destroy   increase/decrease
profit/lose   recover/lose
insert/remove   extend/shorten

9.

10.

11.

12.

READ on your OWN
Great Unsolved Mysteries, pages 10–12

BEFORE YOU READ

Think about the last pages you read in "On Treasure's Trail." Name one explorer who searched for El Dorado and tell about what happened in the search.

AS YOU READ

Preview all the text features in "The Money Pit" and "Digging for Treasure" on pages 10–12 to predict what you will be reading about. (STOP) Complete the first two sentences in the chart below. Then read pages 10–12 and answer the last question.

The Money Pit and *Digging For Treasure*
I predict these sections will be about
To make my prediction, I looked at
Did your prediction match what you read about, or were there any surprises? Explain.

VOCABULARY
Watch for the words you are learning about.

insert: to put something in something else

profit: to gain wealth

FLUENCY
Remember to pause at commas and periods as you read.

AFTER YOU READ

What do you think is the most interesting thing that McGinnis's team found in the Money Pit? Why do you think so?

PREDICT: What You Know

How to Predict

Preview text features to get an idea of what you will be reading about.

Use what you know to predict what will happen next.

Use different skills to **preview fiction and nonfiction**.

Check your predictions. You can confirm them or change your prediction.

Elaborate on your predictions.

Learn the STRATEGY

Good readers make predictions about what will happen next. To make a prediction, think about what you already know. You can draw on your experiences and knowledge. For instance, imagine that you are reading about two men. These men are racing to patent the telephone. You know that Alexander Graham Bell is famous for inventing the telephone, so you can predict that Bell won the race. With that prediction in mind, you can focus more on *how* Bell won. You can also draw on what you've learned so far in what you're reading. The text features and the details and information you have already read can help you to predict what might happen next.

Read the first paragraph below. Stop and write your prediction on the lines for what will happen next. Then finish reading on to the end of the passage.

Randy couldn't wait to start using his new metal detector. He decided to start by searching his front yard. *Who knows what I might find?* he thought, dreaming of everything from old coins to buried treasure. His mother's voice interrupted his thoughts. "Randy! Have you seen my car keys?" (STOP)

Just then, Randy's detector began beeping. Randy swept the device over the grass, but he didn't need a metal detector to find what lay in front of him. There were his mother's car keys, right where she had dropped them on her way from the car to the front door.

Your prediction is

_____

_____

_____

To make your prediction, did you use information you already knew, details in the text, or both? Explain your answer.

_____

_____

_____

Did your prediction match what you read?

_____

_____

_____

→YOUR TURN

Preview the passage and photo. Then read to the end of the first paragraph and answer questions 1 and 2.

1. What do you predict will happen next in John Wesley Huddleston's story?

2. To make your prediction, did you use background knowledge, text features and details in the text, or all these things? Explain your answer.

Finish reading the passage and answer question 3.

3. Was there any information in the passage that you didn't predict? Explain.

"Hard" Luck

A diamond hunter at the park that was once Huddleston's farm

The year was 1906. The place was the farm that John Wesley Huddleston had bought with a down payment of one mule. Trying to turn a **profit** with the sleepy farm, Huddleston was feeding the hogs one day when he noticed flecks of a shiny substance in the greenish mud at his feet. Huddleston **inserted** the substance into a washing pan to wash away the mud. In the bottom of the pan were yellow and white crystals. Deciding to polish the crystals, Huddleston took them to his grinding wheel. However, the crystals were so hard that they made deep tracks in the grinding wheel. (STOP)

Huddleston took the crystals to a local bank president. The president sent them to a jeweler. The farmer learned that he had discovered two high-quality diamonds. It must have taken Huddleston some time to **recover** from his shock. "Diamond John" Huddleston later sold the farm for $36,000. The farm is now a state park in Arkansas. The public can search there for diamonds. It takes about 100 hours to find a diamond, but tourists don't let the slim chances of finding a diamond **defeat** them!

Practice reading difficult sentences in a passage until you can read the entire passage without mistakes.

FLUENCY

READ on your OWN
Great Unsolved Mysteries, pages 13–15

BEFORE YOU READ

Think about the last pages you read in "On Treasure's Trail." Why do you think the hole filled with water?

AS YOU READ

Read "Deeper Into the Pit," page 13. (STOP)
Use what you know to make a prediction about whether the search for the treasure in the pit could continue. Write your prediction in the chart below.

Read "The Challenge Continues," page 14 and "A Clue?" page 15. (STOP)
Complete the two remaining boxes in the chart.

Page 13	Pages 14–15
What I predict	Information I predicted that was in the pages
	Information that was in the pages that I didn't predict

VOCABULARY
Watch for the words you are learning about.

defeat: to beat

inserted: put something into something else

recover: to get back

increase: to become larger in amount

extend: to stretch out in length

profit: to gain wealth

FLUENCY
Practice reading difficult sentences in a passage or section of text until you can read the entire passage or section without mistakes.

AFTER YOU READ

Choose the most interesting part about the search for the treasure in the Money Pit and tell why you think it is interesting.

Make Words Yours!

Learn the WORDS

As you read about treasure, you'll come across these words. This is your chance to get to know them better.

WORD AND EXPLANATION	EXAMPLE	WRITE AN EXAMPLE
Credit is recognition or approval for something done or achieved. You may get extra **credit** for doing additional work at school.	Tamika gave her teammates some of the **credit** for her winning run.	When have you received **credit** for something you did well?
A **historic** place or event is something that is an important part of history.	The Constitution is a **historic** object.	What was a **historic** moment for the United States?
When you **inform**, you give facts or information to someone.	Please **inform** us about tonight's homework.	What has someone **informed** you about recently?
Someone who is in the **military** is in the armed forces, such as the army.	My older brother wants to join the **military** next year.	When have you seen someone who is in the **military**?
To **plunder** is to rob and destroy.	Many valuable items were lost when Egyptian tombs were **plundered**.	What would you do if your room was **plundered**?
The **quantity** of something is how many or how much of it there is.	This container holds a maximum **quantity** of one gallon.	What does your classroom have a large **quantity** of?
When you **refer** to something, you name it or mention it.	In his speech, the mayor **referred** twice to his program for the homeless.	When would you **refer** to someone by using his or her full name?
Things that **revolve** move in a circle around other things.	The Earth takes one year to **revolve** once around the Sun.	What does your life **revolve** around?

→YOUR TURN

Answer these questions and be ready to explain your answers.

1. Is a *quantity* likely to be measured in numbers? _____

2. Can you *refer* to a friend by a nickname? _____

3. Are soldiers in the *military*? _____

4. Can a person *revolve*? _____

Choose the right word

> credit   historic   inform   military
> plunder   quantity   refer   revolve

Fill each blank with the correct word from the box.

5. The city was under the control of the _____.

6. Did you _____ Jim that you were leaving?

7. Tanya would _____ to her brother as her best friend.

8. Be sure to give Maria _____ for helping.

9. The _____ building has stood for more than 200 years.

10. Thieves might _____ a home.

11. The blades of the overhead fan don't _____ properly.

12. There was a large _____ of water in the flooded basement.

Show that you know the words by writing about treasures.

Show that you know

Complete the sentences.

13. A museum might be *plundered* if _____

14. Treasure hunters should get *credit* if they _____

15. A treasure hunter should *inform* _____

16. There could be *historic* treasures where _____

READ on your OWN
Great Unsolved Mysteries, pages 16–19

BEFORE YOU READ

Think about the last pages you read in "On Treasure's Trail." What happened to the carved stone that was found in the Money Pit?

AS YOU READ

Preview pages 16–17 of "Missing Confederate Gold." (STOP)
Use your preview to predict what this section will tell about.

Now, read pages 16–17. (STOP)
Complete the two remaining boxes in the first column.

Preview "The Lost Gold," pages 18–19. (STOP)
Use your preview and what you know about the gold to predict what this section will tell about. Write your prediction in the second column.

Now, read pages 18–19. (STOP)
Complete the two remaining boxes in the second column.

Pages 16–17	Pages 18–19
What I predict	What I predict
Information I predicted that was in the pages	Information I predicted that was in the pages
Information that was in the pages that I didn't predict	Information that was in the pages that I didn't predict

VOCABULARY
Watch for the words you are learning about.

plundered: robbed and spoiled

inform: to give information to someone

quantity: an amount

military: a group of soldiers

FLUENCY
Read in a smooth, relaxed manner, as if you were talking to someone.

AFTER YOU READ

Do you think the tale of Parker's group being robbed is a believable story? Why or why not?

PREDICT: Generating Predictions

How to Predict

Preview text features to get an idea of what you will be reading about.

Use what you know to predict what will happen next.

Use different skills to **preview fiction and nonfiction**.

Check your predictions. You can confirm them or change your prediction.

Elaborate on your predictions.

Learn the STRATEGY

You've learned that good readers make predictions before and during reading to help them understand what they read. To generate, or come up with, a good prediction, you don't just guess. Before you read, you can preview text and ask yourself, *What is this going to be about?* While you read, you can use what you already know in order to make predictions. When you find details and information in the text, you can ask yourself questions about what you have just read. Ask, *What do I already know about this topic? What is likely to happen next? Why do I think that?* The answers to all these questions will help you to come up with good predictions. The more details you use, both before and during reading, the better your prediction will be.

Read the paragraph below.

The paragraph is an introduction to the passage on page 130. Think about what you already know and what is likely to come next. Then predict what the passage on the next page will be about.

I think the passage will be about

_____

_____

_____

My prediction is based on

_____

_____

_____

CIVIL WAR TREASURES

From April 30 to May 6, 1863, Union and Confederate soldiers faced each other in the Battle of Chancellorsville. This site is near Fredricksburg, Virginia. The odds were against the Confederacy. Their army of 60,000 soldiers was led by General Robert E. Lee. They faced 130,000 Union soldiers. The Union soldiers were led by Major General Joseph Hooker. General Lee and his soldiers won the battle by outsmarting the Union soldiers. Today, the battlefield attracts treasure hunters who collect relics from the Civil War. These treasures range from bullets to lost buttons.

YOUR TURN

Preview "The Treasures of Chancellorsville." Use your preview and what you read on the previous page to make another prediction about what the passage will be about. Write your responses for numbers 1 and 2 below.

1. Prediction

2. Your prediction was based on

Read the passage. Then answer number 3.

3. Was there information in the passage that you didn't predict? Explain.

The Treasures of Chancellorsville

Historic Chancellorsville Chancellorsville is a **historic** site. A major battle of the Civil War was fought there. The relics that have been found at the site are important. What kinds of treasure have been found?

All Kinds of Treasures Think about the uniforms of the soldiers. Many buttons and belt buckles were lost during battle. Even small strips of material that decorated the shoulders of their uniforms have been found. These strips are called epaulets.

Treasure seekers have also discovered weapons such as rifles or pistols. Bullets that were never fired have been found. Seekers who find a bayonet—the short blade that attached to the end of the rifle—deserve special **credit**. The tip of the bayonet is often missing from the rifle itself, however. Has it been **plundered**? No. Rather, soldiers sometimes used these weapons for cooking over a campfire, and the tips were lost. Other treasures include spurs, backpack hooks, locks, and money.

People who don't have time to visit battlefields such as Chancellorsville can search for Civil War treasures on the Internet. Various sites **inform** interested buyers about available items. However, treasure seekers would agree that a trip to a battlefield is much more fun and rewarding!

Practice reading sentences with difficult words until you can read them smoothly, without hesitation.

FLUENCY

READ on your OWN
Great Unsolved Mysteries, pages 20–22

BEFORE YOU READ

Think about the last pages you read in "On Treasure's Trail." Who was Captain Parker, and what was he supposed to do with the Confederate gold?

AS YOU READ

Read pages 20–21 of "The Captain's Version" and "Who Lost the Gold?" (STOP)

On the lines below, make a prediction about whether anyone ever discovered what happened to the gold.

_____

_____

_____

Read page 22. (STOP)
Answer the questions.
On the lines below, tell if your prediction matched the text or if you read anything that surprised you.

_____

_____

_____

VOCABULARY
Watch for the words you are learning about.

inform: to give information to someone

credit: praise for something done

quantity: an amount

refer: to talk about

historic: related to an important past event

FLUENCY
Reread the passage to practice reading smoothly and accurately.

AFTER YOU READ

Which of the explanations of what happened to the gold do you think is true? Explain your answer.

Get Wordwise!
Shades of Meaning

Learn More About the WORDS

Many words have similar meanings. However, sometimes one word fits better in a certain situation than another.

The words *increase* and *extend* have similar meanings. Both describe making something bigger. However, *extend* means to make something bigger by making it longer, while *increase* means making it bigger in any way.

The builder had to **extend** the dock another six feet into the water.

In the sentence above, *extend* would be a better choice than *increase* because the dock is being made longer.

WORD AND EXPLANATION	SIMILAR WORD AND EXPLANATION	USE THE WORDS
credit: recognition or approval for an accomplishment	**praise:** compliments or congratulations	Frequent _____ seems to make my little brother behave better. I deserve _____ for studying hard.
revolve: to move in a circle	**turn:** to move in a different direction	Kim said to _____ left at the corner. The planets _____ around the Sun.
plunder: to steal and destroy	**rob:** to take something that belongs to someone else	The man tried to _____ the same bank twice. The police guarded the museum after the war so no one would _____ it.
historic: remembered for its importance in the past	**significant:** important	The new building is _____ because the mayor will have his office there. The cabin is a _____ site because an early settler lived there.
inform: to give facts	**explain:** to make clear and understandable	I need someone to _____ what you learned in science class yesterday. The airline had to _____ the passengers that the flight was delayed.

YOUR TURN

Show that you know about shades of meaning. Use the words below to write about treasures.

Choose the best word

The boldfaced words have similar meanings, but one word fits better than the other. Circle the word that fits best in each sentence.

1. George Washington's home is a **significant / historic** spot.

2. Who deserves the most **credit / praise** for finishing the project on time?

3. The hubcaps on the sports car flash when the tires **revolve / turn**.

4. After their home was **robbed / plundered** our neighbors had to make many repairs.

5. Ryan had to **explain / inform** why he was late for school.

True or False?

Write whether each statement is true or false.

6. Ferris wheels and merry-go-rounds *revolve*. _____

7. The White House is a *historic* place. _____

8. Reading the newspaper is one way to stay *informed*. _____

9. It is wrong to give someone *credit* for something he or she has done. _____

10. All places that are robbed are *plundered*. _____

Show that you know

Choose two of the word pairs. Write a sentence for each word in those pairs.

plunder/rob	revolve/turn
historic/significant	inform/explain
credit/praise	

11.

12.

13.

14.

READ on your OWN
Great Unsolved Mysteries, pages 23–25

BEFORE YOU READ

Think about the last pages you read in "On Treasure's Trail." What did Captain Parker say about the gold?

AS YOU READ

Preview "A Lost Gold Mine," pages 23–25. (STOP)
Use what you know about searching for lost treasure to make two predictions about what will happen in this chapter. Write your predictions in the chart below.

Read pages 23–25. (STOP)
Complete the chart.

Pages 23–25	
I predict	*I also predict*
Information I predicted that was in the chapter	Information I predicted that was in the chapter
Information that was in the chapter that I didn't predict	Information that was in the chapter that I didn't predict

AFTER YOU READ

Which part of the story about the mine in the Superstition Mountains do you think is most interesting? Explain.

PREDICT: Previewing Fiction

How to Predict

Preview text features to get an idea of what you will be reading about.	**Use what you know** to predict what will happen next.	Use different skills to **preview fiction and nonfiction**.	**Check** your predictions. You can confirm them or change your prediction.	**Elaborate** on your predictions.

Learn the STRATEGY

When you read a fiction story or novel, you can use certain text features to help predict what is going to happen. Text features in fiction include the title, chapter heads, and illustrations. You can also look at the table of contents if the novel has one. The table of contents can give you an idea of what the story will be about.

Another good way to make predictions is to skim the story or take a quick look at it before you read. Skimming can show you what some of the key events and characters in the book are.

Contents

CHAPTER 1
A Tale From the Past: Amelia's Gold 7

CHAPTER 2
An Idea Is Born: The Search Begins . . . 18

CHAPTER 3
A First Attempt: Not All Clues Help 26

CHAPTER 4
A Map Is Discovered:
The Search Moves Forward 37

CHAPTER 5
Danger From Below:
The Mine Is not Safe 49

CHAPTER 6
Success at Last: The Gold Is Found 55

Skim the table of contents to the left for *The Path to Amelia's Treasure*.

Circle the best response.

What do you think this book is about?

a. using a map
b. Amelia's adventures
c. searching for Amelia's gold
d. playing in mines

Which chapter heading makes you think there will be a problem?

a. "An Idea Is Born"
b. "A Map Is Discovered"
c. "Danger From Below"
d. "Success at Last"

➤ YOUR TURN

Preview "Finding a Treasure" by skimming the story. Complete questions 1 and 2 below.

FINDING A TREASURE

Maria had found the greatest movie poster at the neighborhood flea market. The leading man wore a **military** uniform and the leading lady was a famous actress. She couldn't wait to frame it and hang it in her room.

Later that night Maria was reading the newspaper. There was an article about a store that sold old movie posters, and this got Maria thinking. Maybe the poster she just bought was valuable. Maria **referred** to the newspaper article again and saw that the article included the name and address of the store. The store was only two subway stops away.

A few days later, Maria carefully rolled up her poster and headed off to the store. Her thoughts **revolved** around all the things she could buy if it turned out her poster was valuable. At the store there was a great **quantity** of movie posters and other items from movies. The storeowner studied Maria's poster, then said, "Sorry, it's only worth five dollars." Maria was so disappointed.

That evening, Maria showed her mother the poster. "That's your dad's favorite movie!" her mother exclaimed.

Maria jumped up. "I know what," she said excitedly. "I'll frame it and give it to him for his birthday next week. See, it's valuable after all!"

1. What did you look at when you skimmed this story?

2. What do you predict will happen in this story?

Read the story and complete question 3.

3. Did anything happen in the story that you didn't predict?

Watch for quotation marks. Read the quoted words as the speaker would say them.

FLUENCY

READ on your OWN
Great Unsolved Mysteries, pages 26–28

BEFORE YOU READ

Think about the last pages you read in "On Treasure's Trail." Why did Weiser and Waltz hide the gold they found?

AS YOU READ

You can skim text to help you make predictions. Also look at the titles, heads, and photos to help with your prediction.

Skim pages 26–27 of "The World's Treasures" and "A Peek Into Long-Ago Worlds." STOP
Write a prediction in the first column of the chart for what these pages are about. Then read pages 26–27, and complete the first column.

Skim "Stolen Art!" page 28. STOP
Write a prediction in the second column of the chart for what this page is about. Then read page 28, and complete the second column.

Pages 26–27	Page 28
What I predict	What I predict
Information I predicted that was in the pages	Information I predicted that was in the page
Information that was in the pages that I didn't predict	Information that was in the page that I didn't predict

AFTER YOU READ

Choose the most interesting page or section. Which type of treasure did you find the most interesting?

PREDICT: Previewing Nonfiction

How to Predict

Preview text features to get an idea of what you will be reading about.	**Use what you know** to predict what will happen next.	Use different skills to **preview fiction and nonfiction**.	**Check** your predictions. You can confirm them or change your prediction.	**Elaborate** on your predictions.

Learn the STRATEGY

Before you begin reading nonfiction, it's a good idea to predict what the passage or chapter might be about. Nonfiction has more features than fiction to preview. These features include the title, heads, subheads, boldfaced words, and any photos, captions, illustrations, charts, maps, and diagrams.

You may also want to skim the text. You skim text by looking through it quickly. This will help you to get a feeling for what it is about.

Preview "History of Gold" by looking at text features and skimming. Then follow the directions on the right side of this page.

HISTORY OF GOLD

First Used Early people may have picked gold off the ground as long ago as 40,000 BCE. There is evidence that people were using gold by 4000 BCE in Central and Eastern Europe. The Egyptians had become experts at using gold by 3000 BCE. They beat gold into very thin layers. Then they used it to make jewelry.

Used as Money Gold has been used as a form of money for many years. About 1500 BCE a coin called the shekel was used for currency in many areas of the Middle East. This coin was two-thirds gold and one-third silver. In 50 BCE, the Romans used a gold coin called the aureus. The first gold coin in the United States was made in 1787.

Circle two predictions for what the passage is about.

a. Silver has lots of uses.
b. Gold was first used long ago.
c. Gold is used as medicine.
d. Gold is used as money.

Now read the passage. How did previewing and skimming the text help you make your predictions?

_____
_____
_____
_____

Preview "King Tut" by looking at text features and by skimming the passage. Complete numbers 1 and 2 below. Then read the passage and complete number 3.

SOCIAL STUDIES CONNECTION

King Tut

Finding King Tut Not all pharaohs were buried in pyramids. The pharaoh Tutankhamun was buried in a modest tomb. Tutankhamun, **referred** to as King Tut, died when he was very young. For more than 3,000 years, the location of his tomb was unknown.

A Long Search An Englishman named Howard Carter was determined to find King Tut's tomb. He and his partner, Lord Carnarvon, searched for eight years. By 1922, they were ready to give up. In one final effort, Carter started digging in a new spot. This time he found a staircase that led downward to a door. Behind the door was an untouched tomb filled with priceless objects.

An Amazing Find Most Egyptian tombs had been **plundered** over the years. However, King Tut's tomb hadn't been opened since the king's burial. This made Carter's discovery **historic**. Reporters quickly informed the world about King Tut's tomb.

Treasures From the Past When the tomb was opened, workers found a large **quantity** of gold, jewels, and lovely furniture. The biggest treasure of all was a solid gold coffin. It held the mummified body of King Tut. Today these objects are on display at the Egyptian Museum in Cairo for everyone to enjoy.

1. What clues did you get by previewing and skimming the passage?

2. Make three predictions about what you will learn from the passage.

3. Were your predictions helpful? Why?

Skim the passage for words that are unfamiliar or hard to pronounce. Practice reading those words ahead of time.

FLUENCY

READ on your OWN
Great Unsolved Mysteries, pages 29–31

BEFORE YOU READ

Think about the last pages you read in "On Treasure's Trail." Why do people steal important art pieces?

AS YOU READ

Skim "Found Treasure" and "Missing Treasure," pages 29–30. (STOP)
Write two predictions in the first column of the chart for what these pages are about. Then read pages 29–30 and complete the first column.

Skim "Treasure Belongs to Everyone," page 31. (STOP)
Write a prediction in the second column of the chart for what this page is about and complete the second column.

VOCABULARY
Watch for the words you are learning about.

revolving: moving in a circle or orbit

historic: having, or likely to have, lasting importance

informing: giving facts or knowledge to people

FLUENCY
Be careful to read every word without skipping or substituting words.

Pages 29–30	Page 31
My two predictions	My prediction
Information I predicted that was in the pages	Information I predicted that was in the page
Information that was in the pages that I didn't predict	Information that was in the page that I didn't predict

AFTER YOU READ

Which of the art objects mentioned in this book would you most like to see?

Make Words Yours!

Learn the WORDS

Here are some words you will be reading in the next week. They are also words you need to know for your everyday reading.

WORD AND EXPLANATION	EXAMPLE	WRITE AN EXAMPLE
When you **analyze** something, you examine it carefully.	The detective **analyzed** the evidence to look for clues.	What have you **analyzed** recently?
If something is **atypical**, it is unusual, or not normal. **Typical** describes something that is normal.	It's usually hot in the summer, so this cool weather is **atypical**.	What is an **atypical** food to eat for dinner?
A **concept** is an idea.	We brainstormed to come up with **concepts** for our stories.	What new **concept** have you learned lately?
Construction is the act of making or building something. Something that has been built is a **construction**.	The **construction** of the museum is expected to take over a year.	What **construction** have you seen lately?
When you **debate**, you argue for or against something. A **debate** is a discussion in which you argue for or against something.	We **debated** whether or not the new cafeteria rules were fair.	What is a topic you might **debate** with your friends?
A **fragment** is a piece of something.	When I dropped the glass, it shattered into **fragments**.	What might you find a **fragment** of?
Things that are **identical** are exactly the same.	Tony and Tim are **identical** twins.	What else can be **identical**?
Something **impressive** has a strong effect on you, usually very positive.	The huge new school auditorium is certainly **impressive**.	What is something that you find **impressive**?

→ YOUR TURN

Yes or No?

Answer these questions and be ready to explain your answers.

1. Is crying *atypical* behavior for small babies? _____

2. Are apples and oranges *identical*? _____

3. Is a museum a *construction*? _____

4. Can you *debate* a *concept*? _____

Choose the right word

> analyze   concept   debate   construction
> atypical   fragment   identical   impressive

Fill each blank with the correct word.

5. The swimming champion has an [_____] record.

6. DNA is a difficult [_____] for some people to understand.

7. Tim's shirt is [_____] to mine!

8. We started to [_____] the motives of the characters in the novel.

9. Candidates [_____] the issues.

10. We don't usually get much homework, but yesterday was [_____].

11. The builders put up a fence to keep children away from the [_____].

12. Miguel overheard a [_____] of the conversation.

How would you go about solving a mystery? Show that you know the words by finishing the sentences.

Show that you know

Complete the sentences.

13. I would *analyze* _____

14. A clue might be a *fragment* of _____

15. I might get into a *debate* about _____

16. It would be *impressive* if I _____

READ on your OWN
Great Unsolved Mysteries, pages 32–35

BEFORE YOU READ

Think about what you know about mysteries of history. Why do you think people would want to solve mysteries that happened long ago?

AS YOU READ

COMPREHENSION

Skim pages 32–34 of "Uncovering History's Secrets." (STOP)
Write two predictions in the first column of the chart for what these pages are about. Then read pages 32–34, and complete the first column.

Skim "Secrets of Stonehenge," page 35. (STOP)
Write a prediction in the second column of the chart for what this page is about. Then read page 35, and complete the second column.

Pages 32–34	Page 35
My two predictions	My prediction
Information I predicted that was in the pages	Information I predicted that was in the page
Information that was in the pages that I didn't predict	Information that was in the page that I didn't predict

VOCABULARY

Watch for the words you are learning about.

impressive: describing something that is wonderful

reconstruct: to build again

debate: to argue for or against

FLUENCY

To make sense of the text, watch for commas and read phrases as short sentences.

AFTER YOU READ

Choose the most interesting mystery of history mentioned in "Uncovering History's Secrets." Write a question you hope will be answered when you read on.

↓ PREDICT: Checking Yourself

How to Predict

| **Preview text features** to get an idea of what you will be reading about. | **Use what you know** to predict what will happen next. | Use different skills to **preview fiction and nonfiction**. | **Check** your predictions. You can confirm them or change your prediction. | **Elaborate** on your predictions. |

Learn the STRATEGY

After you decide what you think is going to happen in the text and what you will be reading about, keep your predictions in mind as you read. Check each prediction to see if it matches the text. Ask, *Does my prediction go along with what I am reading?* Good readers always check to make sure that their predictions match what they are reading.

Checking your predictions helps you know whether or not you understand what you read. What can you do when you realize that your prediction is different from the text? You can reread the text to look for clues that you might have missed. Identifying missed information will help you revise, or change, your prediction.

Read the following passage.

THE CHINESE EMPEROR'S SOLUTION

A Great Wall The Great Wall of China stretches almost 4,000 miles across China. This wall was built from dirt, stone, and brick. So who deserves the credit for this amazing project?

Worry About Enemies More than 2,000 years ago, there were few people living in northern China. The emperor worried that enemies would invade from the north. Shorter walls along the country's borders already existed. This Chinese emperor wanted to connect the walls to make one long wall large enough to keep out enemy forces.

The short passage you just read is an introduction to a longer passage on page 145. Use the information in the short passage to predict what the longer passage will be about. Make two predictions.

_____

_____

_____

_____

_____

_____

_____

Read "The Great Wall of China." Check your predictions as you read, and revise them if necessary. Then answer the questions below.

The Great Wall of
CHINA

A New Concept

The emperor knew the wall had to be large. To show the **concept** of the wall, he used horses and men as measurements. He wanted it to be six horses wide at the top, eight horses wide at the bottom, and five men high. The Great Wall of China is also very long. In fact, it is the longest structure ever built and one of the most **impressive**.

Forced Work

The **construction** was done by hand by more than 1 million Chinese workers. They were simply forced to march north, where they worked night and day. The workers weren't given a chance to **debate** whether they would work on the wall. Anyone foolish enough to complain or try to escape was killed. Many workers spent their entire adult lives building the wall. However, their incredible effort paid off. For more than 1,000 years, the wall kept China safe from its enemies.

1. Did your first prediction on page 144 match the text, or did you have to revise it as you read? Explain.

2. Did your second prediction on page 144 match the text, or did you have to revise it as you read? Explain.

Keep up your pace to maintain interest. Explain events as if you were a part of them.

FLUENCY

READ on your OWN
Great Unsolved Mysteries, pages 36–38

VOCABULARY
Watch for the words you are learning about.

fragments: pieces

constructed: built

construction: the act of building

analyze: to examine carefully

concept: an idea

FLUENCY
Read in a conversational tone, as if you were speaking to a friend.

BEFORE YOU READ

Think about the last pages you read in "Mysteries of History." Where is Stonehenge and what makes it special?

AS YOU READ

Checking your predictions as you read will help you know whether or not you are understanding the text. As you read, remember to ask, *Does my prediction go along with what I am reading about?*

Preview "Constructing Stonehenge," pages 36–38. Then read the first paragraph on page 36. (STOP)
Use what you know to predict what this section will be about. Write your prediction in the chart below.

Now read pages 36–38. (STOP)
Complete the chart.

Preview, read, and predict	Read and check
I predict "Constructing Stonehenge" will be about	**Did your prediction match the text, or did you have to revise it? Explain.**

AFTER YOU READ

Which of the theories about Stonehenge do you find most interesting? Explain.

Get Wordwise!
Word Families

Learn More About the WORDS

A **word family** is a group of words that are related because they all come from the same base word. Here is an example of a word family.

base word: act

some other words in the family: action, activity, actor, acting

Use what you know about the vocabulary word at the top of each box to choose the correct meaning of the other words in the same word family.

ANALYZE

To **analyze** is to study carefully.

An **analysis** of a subject
- ☐ looks at all the parts.
- ☐ is a short study.

An **analytical** person is usually
- ☐ fast.
- ☐ careful.

CONSTRUCTION

Construction is the act of making or building something.

To **construct** something is to
- ☐ put it together.
- ☐ take it apart.

A **constructive** comment is intended to
- ☐ make things worse.
- ☐ be helpful.

IMPRESSIVE

Something that is **impressive** is wonderful or admirable.

When you **impress** someone, you
- ☐ are ignored.
- ☐ are noticed.

If you are **impressionable**, you
- ☐ are affected by things.
- ☐ don't notice things.

INFORM

To **inform** is to give facts to someone.

To give **information** is to
- ☐ tell true things.
- ☐ make up a story.

An **informative** article
- ☐ makes you laugh.
- ☐ teaches you something.

CONCEPT

A **concept** is an idea.

When something is in the **conceptual** stage, it is
- ☐ still being thought about.
- ☐ being done.

An inventor **conceptualizes**
- ☐ the way things were done before.
- ☐ a new idea.

IDENTICAL

Identical means exactly the same.

An **identification** card shows
- ☐ that you live in a city.
- ☐ that you are the person you say you are.

Your **identity** is
- ☐ who you are.
- ☐ what you look like.

→ YOUR TURN

Which word works?

Circle the word in each pair that fits best in the sentence.

1. The book gave me all the **informative / information** I needed for my report.

2. The class president's speech was very **informative / information**.

3. Tonia tried to **impress / impressionable** me with her singing.

4. The Empire State Building is an **impressive / impressionable** sight!

5. Max's teacher gave him lots of **construction / constructive** criticism.

6. They are raising money to **construct / construction** a new museum.

7. Julie is a very **analysis / analytical** person.

8. Tori had to show **identity / identification** papers to enter the country.

9. The fingerprints proved the **identity / identification** of the thief.

10. It is hard to **conceptual / conceptualize** a world without electricity.

Choose the right word

identity informative construct conceptual

Fill each blank with the correct word.

11. The town is going to _____ a playground near my house.

12. My book is in the _____ stage. I am still deciding on the plot.

13. We watched an _____ show about space travel.

14. I don't know the _____ of the person who sent me flowers.

You've read about mysterious places. Use the words below to write about them.

Show that you know

Answer the questions. Use sentences.

15. What *impresses* you most about mysterious places?

16. What place would you like to do an *analysis* of?

READ on your OWN
Great Unsolved Mysteries, pages 39–41

Great Unsolved Mysteries, pages 39–41

BEFORE YOU READ

Think about the last pages you read in "Mysteries of History." What are some of the ideas about who built Stonehenge?

AS YOU READ

Preview pages 39–41. Then read all of page 39. 🛑
Use what you know after previewing these pages and after reading page 39 to make two predictions about what will come next. Then fill in the chart below.

Read pages 40–41. 🛑
Answer the question in the chart.

VOCABULARY
Watch for the words you are learning about.

conceptualized: thought of

identical: same

constructed: built

atypical: not normal

FLUENCY
Read in a smooth, relaxed manner, pausing after phrases as you would if you were having a conversation.

Page 39	Pages 40–41
What I know	Did your predictions match what you read about, or did you have to make revisions? Explain.
My predictions	

AFTER YOU READ

Choose a page and tell about something on that page that surprised you.

↓ PREDICT: Changing Your Mind

How to Predict

Preview text features to get an idea of what you will be reading about.

Use what you know to predict what will happen next.

Use different skills to **preview fiction and nonfiction**.

Check your predictions. You can confirm them or change your prediction.

Elaborate on your predictions.

Learn the STRATEGY

What do you do when you check a prediction you have made and it doesn't match what you've read? You change your mind. Predictions can change as the author reveals new information.

Sometimes authors don't give enough clues to make a good prediction because they want to keep you in suspense. Many mystery writers do this. So do some nonfiction writers. Writers of some kinds of nonfiction, such as the history of a true event, have a story to tell. They don't want to give away the ending. These are some of the reasons why you might need to change a prediction as you continue reading.

Read the passage below and make a prediction about what will happen next in Zeugma. The passage will be continued on the next page.

UNCOVERING ZEUGMA

The city of Zeugma once lay on the banks of the Euphrates River in Turkey. Founded more than 2,000 years ago, the ancient city was a military base for the Roman Empire. It was a bustling center for trade with China. The people who lived in Zeugma had beautiful homes decorated with mosaics and statues. As the centuries passed, Zeugma was abandoned, and people forgot about it. Then, in the 1990s, archaeologists discovered the ruins of Zeugma. However, the amazing find was already under a great threat. Turkey was planning to build a dam that would flood the area. The flooding would help local farmers water their land. Had Zeugma been uncovered only to be buried again?

What do you predict will happen next to the treasures of Zeugma?

_____

_____

_____

What details did you use to make your prediction?

_____

_____

_____

Read the first paragraph of "Saving Zeugma." Then look back at your prediction on page 150 and answer the first question below.

> **1.** Does your prediction match the text, or do you want to revise it? Explain.

Read the rest of "Saving Zeugma." Then answer the question in the box below.

> **2.** Was there information in the text that you did not expect? Explain.

Saving Zeugma

After word spread about the flooding of the ruins at Zeugma, many archaeologists had an **identical** reaction. They raced to the site. They were determined to preserve as many treasures as they could before the city disappeared under the floodwaters. Their response was not **atypical** in the world of archaeology. International teams often work together at a site. 🛑

A Difficult Job

Not all the ruins would be underwater after the dam was built. So archaeologists decided to dig only in the areas that would be flooded. Much of the ancient town was buried under dirt and sand. Archaeologists used radar to **analyze** where buildings had once stood. They could start digging after they had this information.

The Treasures of Zeugma

Many objects were discovered in the ruins. Diggers found **fragments** and complete examples of helmets, spears, pots, coins, jewelry, and tiles. Today the places where these treasures were found are underwater. Finds that were lost include a newly uncovered 14-room house. However, archaeologists are still working in the parts of the historic town that were not flooded.

Read with expression. By using expression, you will be able to understand more of what you read.

FLUENCY

READ on your OWN
Great Unsolved Mysteries, pages 42–44

BEFORE YOU READ

Think about the last pages you read in "Mysteries of History."
What are Moai?

AS YOU READ

Preview pages 42–44. Then read "Walking Home" and
"Mysterious Moai," pages 42–43. (STOP)
Write a prediction in the chart below about what you think
you will learn in "Researching the Moai."

Read "Researching the Moai," page 44. (STOP)
Answer the question in the chart below.

VOCABULARY
Watch for the words you are
learning about.

fragment: to break

debates: discussions

analyzed: examined carefully

typical: normal

impressed: affected deeply

FLUENCY
Read with expression. Reading with
expression will help you
understand what you are reading.

Researching the Moai	
Prediction	Did your prediction match what you read, or did you need to revise it?

AFTER YOU READ

Would you like to visit Easter Island and see the Moai statues?

PREDICT: Elaborating on Predictions With Nonfiction

How to Predict

Preview text features to get an idea of what you will be reading about.	**Use what you know** to predict what will happen next.	Use different skills to **preview fiction and nonfiction**.	**Check** your predictions. You can confirm them or change your prediction.	**Elaborate** on your predictions.

Learn the STRATEGY

When reading nonfiction, good readers use what they have read and what they know to predict what information they may learn next. To generate, or make, a prediction, ask, *What do I already know about this topic?* and *What have I learned already?* To make an even better prediction, add more details. When you add more details, you do what is known as elaboration.

Think about a student who is reading the first chapter in a book about dogs. The student might predict, "This chapter is on the life cycle of dogs." A good reader would take this prediction a step further, and say, "This chapter is on the life cycle of dogs. It's probably about the different stages the dog goes through from being a puppy to being an adult." Elaborating on predictions is a good way to keep you interested in what you are reading—and to help you understand what you read.

Read the paragraph below. Then follow the directions on the right side of this page.

Many people have known about the Sahara Desert and lived in it or near it for ages. However, the same cannot be said for Antarctica. The continent has only been explored in the past few centuries. The earliest explorers who tried to find it were unsuccessful.

The paragraph you just read introduces the passage on page 154. Circle the best simple prediction for what you think the passage will be about.

a. It will be about the exploration of Antarctica.

b. It will be about why deserts have little rain.

c. It will be about why the Sahara is a desert.

Now think about the last sentence of the paragraph and how it might lead to more information about Antarctica. Write a more elaborate prediction about what the passage on page 154 will be about.

_____
_____
_____
_____

➡ YOUR TURN

Preview "The Search for an Unknown Land." Be sure to skim the text for details. Complete the first box below. Then read the passage and answer question 2.

The Search for an Unknown Land

The ancient Greeks wrote about an unknown land in the southernmost part of the world. Greek mapmakers even included this land on their maps.

The continent became known as Terra Australis. For centuries, people **debated** the **concept** of its existence. Some believed Terra Australis was a civilized land. On the other hand, some insisted that the continent was a myth.

In 1772, English explorer James Cook began an **impressive** journey. His mission was to find Terra Australis. In December, Cook and his crew encountered an iceberg. In January, the frozen sea forced Cook to sail north. These events convinced Captain Cook that Terra Australis did not exist. In fact, the cold temperatures proved that people could never live in the region.

Today we know that Captain Cook almost reached Antarctica. Ice kept Cook from getting close enough to see land. Like Cook, others tried to locate the land near the South Pole. However, it was more than 50 years before anyone succeeded.

1. Based on your preview of this passage, make a prediction about what you will be reading. Be sure to elaborate on your prediction by using details.

2. How did elaborating on your prediction help you understand what you read?

> **Use expression as you read to emphasize points that are interesting.**

FLUENCY

READ on your OWN
Great Unsolved Mysteries, pages 45–48

BEFORE YOU READ

Think about the last pages you read in "Mysteries of History."
What did the two researchers do with the statues on Easter Island?

AS YOU READ

Preview pages 45–48 of "Lost Colony of Roanoke." Then read
pages 45–46. (STOP)
Write a prediction in the chart below for what you think will
happen in "Return to Roanoke," pages 47–48. Be sure to elaborate
on your prediction.

Read "Return to Roanoke," pages 47–48. (STOP)
Answer the question in the chart.

Return to Roanoke	
Prediction	Did your prediction match what you read about, or did you have to revise your prediction? Explain.

VOCABULARY
Watch for the words you are learning about.

impressed: affected deeply

construct: to build

fragments: pieces

identical: same

constructed: built

typically: normally

FLUENCY
Vary your expression as you read to make your reading sound smoother and more interesting.

AFTER YOU READ

Which of the places described in "Mysteries of History" so far would you most like to visit?

Make Words Yours!

Learn the WORDS

As you read about other treasure hunts, you'll come across these words. This is your chance to get to know them better.

WORD AND EXPLANATION	EXAMPLE	WRITE AN EXAMPLE
If you **continue** doing something, you keep doing it.	The hikers **continued** on the trail instead of turning back.	Why might you **continue** to do something all day?
Someone's **descendant** is his or her child, grandchild, and so on.	Many Americans are the **descendants** of immigrants who came to this country in the 1800s.	Should all **descendants** keep their family name?
An **image** is a picture or likeness of something. Photographs and statues are both **images**.	Seeing the **images** of Yellowstone National Park made me want to visit it.	What **image** comes to your mind when you hear the word *freedom*?
An **incident** is something that happens. An event is an **incident**.	Were there any witnesses to the **incident**?	What is an **incident** you have described to someone recently?
To be **inclined** means to lean toward something or have a preference for it.	I am **inclined** to believe that he is telling the truth.	Are you more **inclined** to go to the movies or to a concert?
If you **influence** someone or something, you affect that person or the way something happens.	Todd's example **influenced** me to try to become a better ball player.	Who has **influenced** you the most?
Something that is **massive** is huge and often covers a large area.	The White House is a **massive** building in Washington, D.C.	What is another building you would describe as **massive**?
If you are **tempted**, you are persuaded to do something, often against your better judgment.	On hot days, I am often **tempted** to have an ice cream cone instead of lunch.	What else might you be **tempted** to do on a hot day?

→YOUR TURN

Which word makes sense?

Circle the best answer to each question.

1. Which might a thirsty person be *tempted* by?
   lemonade or **crackers**

2. Which is an *incident*?
   an accident or **a bicycle**

3. Which is *massive*?
   a book or **a building**

4. Who would be your *descendants*?
   your children or **your grandparents**

Choose the right word

> continue   descendant   image   incident
> inclined   influence   massive   tempted

Fill each blank with the correct word.

5. That man is a _____ of George Washington.

6. After my alarm goes off, I always _____ to sleep.

7. The magazine has an amazing _____ of underwater life.

8. My absentminded brother is _____ to forget to do his homework.

9. The accident was an unfortunate _____.

10. Most mountains are _____.

11. How much does television _____ you?

12. I was _____ to go to the mall, but I did my homework instead.

Show that you know the words by writing about mysterious places.

Show that you know

Complete the sentences.

13. In a mysterious place, I would be *inclined* to _____

14. A mysterious place may *influence* me if _____

15. A mysterious place I have a strong mental *image* of is _____

16. I will *continue* to think about _____

READ on your OWN
Great Unsolved Mysteries, pages 49–51

BEFORE YOU READ

Think about the last pages you read in "Mysteries of History." Where was the Roanoke Colony and where were the people who settled it from?

AS YOU READ

After you have started to read a nonfiction text, you may want to elaborate on your prediction.

Think about what you read on pages 45–48. Then skim "Gone!" on pages 49–50. (STOP)

Write a prediction for what you think will happen in "Gone!" Be sure to elaborate on the prediction.

_____

_____

_____

Read "Gone!" on pages 49–50. Skim "Theories" on pages 50–51. (STOP)

Write a prediction for what you will read about in "Theories." Be sure to elaborate on the prediction. Then read pages 50–51.

_____

_____

_____

Did elaborating on your predictions help you to better understand the text?

_____

_____

AFTER YOU READ

Which of the theories about Roanoke Island do you think is the best, and why?

VOCABULARY
Watch for the words you are learning about.

continued: kept going

descendants: people who are born to a particular ancestor

influence: an effect on the way something happens

inclined: tended to think in a certain way

FLUENCY
To keep your reading smooth, read phrases as short sentences.

PREDICT: Elaborating on Predictions With Fiction

How to Predict

Preview text features to get an idea of what you will be reading about.

Use what you know to predict what will happen next.

Use different skills to **preview fiction and nonfiction**.

Check your predictions. You can confirm them or change your prediction.

Elaborate on your predictions.

Learn the STRATEGY

Fiction readers, like nonfiction readers, can make better predictions by elaborating on their predictions. When you elaborate, you add more details to a prediction by using what you know. Ask, *What do I think will happen next based on what has already happened?* You can put yourself in the main character's situation and ask, *What would I do if I were the main character?*

Say that a student predicts, "This story is about a little girl who meets a wolf." A good predictor would then ask, *So what happens when she meets the wolf? Why do I think that?* Because of what you know about children and about wolves, you might predict, "Children are afraid of wolves, so I think she would try to run away." You could elaborate on that prediction by asking what would happen if she didn't get away. Elaborating on predictions will help you understand what you are reading.

Read the following passage.

ABOVE THE NORTHERN LIGHTS

Far above Earth's surface, astronaut Miles Manka gazed out the window of the space shuttle. A strange light was breaking in the distance. As the shuttle moved closer, he watched in awe as shimmering curtains of light swayed beneath him.

It was his first sight of the northern lights from space, and it was more beautiful than he'd ever imagined. He thought of his nephew Max. "Max is camping in Montana. I hope that he doesn't miss this spectacular sight!"

"Above the Northern Lights" is an introduction to the passage on page 160. Think about the title and what you've read. Pay attention to how this passage ends. What do you think would logically follow? Use what you know to make a prediction about the next passage.

I think the next passage will be about _____

_____

_____

Ask a question that will make you think further about, or elaborate on, your prediction.

_____

_____

_____

➡ YOUR TURN

Preview "Lights in the Wilderness" and read to the stop sign. Then stop and complete numbers 1 and 2 below.

1. What I know

2. What will happen next? Elaborate on your prediction using details from the story.

Finish reading the passage and complete number 3 below.

3. Was there anything in the story that surprised you?

Lights in the WILDERNESS

Max wasn't thrilled about camping in the wilderness of northern Montana. The only illumination was a sliver of moon in the night sky, a sprinkling of stars, and the light of a campfire. Once the fire fizzled out, Max crawled into the tent and shut out all the **images**. He wasn't **inclined** to relax until he heard his mother slip into her sleeping bag.

A few hours later, Max awoke. The darkness was less intense, but a strange glow filled the tent. Max wanted to huddle deeper into his sleeping bag. Then he realized his mother was gone. Max immediately thought of an **incident** years ago when he got lost in the woods. He hoped his mother hadn't gone far. (STOP)

Max gasped when he stepped outside and saw green lights wavering and wiggling. They formed eerie, cloudlike streaks from ground to sky. "What is it?" he asked.

"The aurora borealis," his mother replied, "also known as the northern lights. They're caused by energy from the Sun. Now sit down and enjoy the show."

The "show" had a powerful **influence** over Max. For the entire hour that he watched, Max marveled at this rare sight. He thought of his uncle Miles, who was on a space mission. "It's too bad Uncle Miles couldn't be here to see this," he said wistfully.

Watch for quotation marks and read the quoted words as the speaker would say them.

READ on your OWN
Great Unsolved Mysteries, pages 52–54

BEFORE YOU READ

Think about the last pages you read in "Mysteries of History." What is one of the theories about why the Roanoke Colony disappeared?

AS YOU READ

Read page 52 of "Strange Zone of the Bermuda Triangle." 🛑
In the chart below, predict what you will learn about in the rest of the chapter. Be sure to elaborate on your prediction by using details in the text.

Read "Other Unexplained Events," page 53, and "Just a Legend?" page 54. 🛑
Answer the question in the chart.

VOCABULARY
Watch for the words you are learning about.

descend: to go down

images: photographs or things that represent something

continued: went on happening

incident: an event

tempting: thinking strongly about something

massive: huge

inclining: leaning a certain way

FLUENCY
Change the expression in your voice to reflect whether information is surprising, serious, or descriptive.

Page 52	*Pages 53–54*
Prediction	Did your prediction match what you read about, or did you need to revise it? Explain.

AFTER YOU READ

Which of the theories about what happens in the Bermuda Triangle do you find most interesting? Why do you think so?

Get Wordwise!
The Suffixes *-ness* and *-ation*

Learn More About the WORDS

You already know that a **suffix** is a word ending and that it changes a word's meaning. Adding the suffix *-ness* or the suffix *-ation* makes a word mean the state of being. The new word is always a noun.

kind<u>ness</u> = the state of being kind

starv<u>ation</u> = the state of being starved

When you add *-ation* to a word that ends in *e*, drop the *e* before you add the suffix: continu<u>e</u>—continu<u>ation</u>.

WORD AND EXPLANATION	ADD *-ness* TO THE WORD	WRITE AN EXAMPLE
Massive means huge.	When we got near the mountain, its _____ surprised us.	When has the **massiveness** of something surprised you?
Something **destructive** wrecks things and can hurt people.	The _____ of the tidal wave was shown all over the world.	What is an example of a puppy's **destructiveness**?

WORD AND EXPLANATION	ADD *-ation* TO THE WORD	WRITE AN EXAMPLE
A **fragment** is a piece of something.	The _____ of the concrete led to the building's collapse.	What could you do to cause **fragmentation** of a rock?
To **continue** means to go on or to keep doing something.	Tomorrow's paper will have the _____ of the article.	Why would there be a **continuation** of a meeting?
To **incline** is to lean toward something or have a preference for it.	Katie had a strong _____ to go to the party anyway.	What kind of movies do you have an **inclination** for?
To **tempt** is to try to convince someone to do something he or she shouldn't do.	I shouldn't watch TV before I do my homework, but this show is a _____.	What foods are a **temptation** for you?

Choose the right word

massiveness   destructiveness   fragmentation
continuation   inclination   temptation

Fill each blank with the correct word from the box.

1. I am looking forward to the _____ of the story.

2. I had a terrible _____ to tell Laura your secret.

3. The _____ of the storm ruined many houses.

4. The _____ of rocks over long periods of time creates sand.

5. After she struck out three times, my sister fought an _____ to quit the team.

6. The _____ of the large building looked odd in the small town.

> Think about what you have read in this unit. Then write about some things you have learned.

Show that you know

Write four sentences. In each, use one of the words from the box.

massiveness   destructiveness   fragmentation
continuation   inclination   temptation

7.

8.

9.

10.

READ on your OWN
Great Unsolved Mysteries, pages 55–57

VOCABULARY
Watch for the words you are learning about.

tempted: attracted to do something

massive: huge

FLUENCY
Read in a smooth, relaxed manner, as if you are telling a story.

BEFORE YOU READ

Think about the last pages you read in "Mysteries of History." What is one of the mysterious incidents that occurred within the Bermuda Triangle?

AS YOU READ

Read page 55 of "Atlantis: Fact or Fiction?"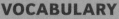
In the chart below, predict what you will learn about in the next section, "Search for Atlantis." Be sure to elaborate on your prediction by using details in the text.

Read "Search for Atlantis," pages 56–57.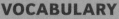
Answer the question in the chart.

Search for Atlantis	
Prediction	**Did your prediction match what you read about, or did you need to revise it? Explain.**

AFTER YOU READ

Which theory about the location of Atlantis do you find most interesting? Why?

PREDICT: Putting It All Together

How to Predict

Preview text features to get an idea of what you will be reading about.

Use what you know to predict what will happen next.

Use different skills to **preview fiction and nonfiction**.

Check your predictions. You can confirm them or change your prediction.

Elaborate on your predictions.

Learn the STRATEGY

You have learned what good readers do when they make predictions about what they are reading. Before you read, you know that to make predictions, you preview the text and think about what you know about the topic. As you read, you think about what might happen next based on what you've already read. You can also use your experiences to think about what might happen next. To make even better predictions, you can elaborate on what you think will happen. Remember to check your predictions to make sure that they match the text. If not, you may need to revise your prediction.

Preview the illustration below. Then follow the directions on this page.

Daily Tribune

NEW ECOSYSTEMS DICOVERED

SCIENTISTS CHANGE THEIR MINDS

Several months ago, marine scientists made an unexpected discovery at the bottom of the ocean. While exploring an underwater mountain range, they discovered an independent ecosystem. More expeditions followed.

An ecosystem is made up of all the animals, plants, and bacteria that live together in a certain environment. The ecosystems that marine scientists have discovered thrive without sunlight. How is that possible?

Based on your preview, make a prediction about the passage. Include the kind of information you used to make your prediction.

I predict that the passage will be about _____

_____

_____

_____

_____

Read the passage. Was your prediction correct? Explain.

_____

_____

_____

The passage on this page introduces the newspaper article that appears on page 166. Make a prediction for what you will learn about in the article.

_____

_____

_____

►YOUR TURN

Preview "Surviving the Sea" and read the first paragraph. Then stop and fill in the first box below.

....
: **1.** Details I can use to make a
: prediction
:
:
:
:
:
:
:
....

In box 2, predict what the rest of the article is about.

....
: **2.** *I predict the article will tell*
: *about*
:
:
:
:
:
:
....

Read the rest of the article. Then answer the question in box 3.

SURVIVING THE SEA

Some creatures and their **descendants** live in places where scientists once thought nothing could survive. Scientists have been studying life in areas near hydrothermal vents. These vents are underwater openings in the earth's crust. They allow steam, boiling hot water, and poisonous gases and chemicals to escape from inside the earth. As a result, they create harsh conditions for living things. 🛑

At one time, scientists were **tempted** to think that nothing could live near these vents. After all, there is no sunlight deep in the **massive** ocean. That means there are no plants. The food chain depends on fragments of plants. The plant fragments feed tiny ocean creatures. These creatures are then eaten by larger animals.

Several deep-sea expeditions have caused scientists to change their

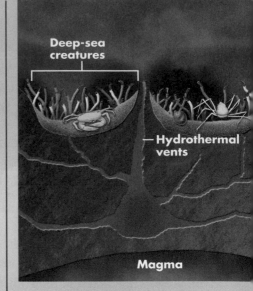

Deep-sea creatures

Hydrothermal vents

Magma

minds. Scientists have now identified and taken photos of more than 300 species of animals that live near the vents. They include strange types of fish, shrimp, crabs, snails, and clams.

What do these sea creatures eat? The tiniest creatures **continue** to survive by eating chemicals from the vents. Snails and crabs eat these tiny animals. Then larger animals complete the food chain by eating the snails and crabs.

....
: **3.** Think back to your first prediction on page 165. Did you have to
: revise your prediction as you read the rest of the article? Explain.
:
:
:
....

┌─────────────────────────┐
│ **Take your time when** │
│ **reading, so you can** │
│ **make sense of** │
│ **difficult ideas.** FLUENCY │
└─────────────────────────┘

READ on your OWN
Great Unsolved Mysteries, pages 58–60

BEFORE YOU READ

Think about the last pages you read in "Mysteries of History." What do you think happened to Atlantis?

AS YOU READ

Read pages 58–59, up to "Connections." **(STOP)**
In the chart below, predict what you think you will learn about in the section "Connections." Be sure to elaborate on your prediction.

Read pages 59–60. **(STOP)**
Answer the question in the chart.

Pages 58–59	*Pages 59–60*
Prediction	Did your prediction match what you read about, or did you need to revise it? Explain.

VOCABULARY
Watch for the words you are learning about.

imagery: descriptions

descendants: people who are born to a particular ancestor

continue: to keep happening

tempted: attracted to do something

FLUENCY
Read in a smooth, relaxed manner, pausing after phrases as you would in conversation.

AFTER YOU READ

If you could solve one of the mysteries that you've read about, which one would it be? Why would you choose that one?

Unit 3 Reflection

VOCABULARY

The easiest part of learning new words is

The hardest part is

I still need to work on

Some interesting words I learned are

Great Unsolved Mysteries

COMPREHENSION

The hardest thing about making predictions is

One prediction hint that has helped me make better predictions is

One hint I need to practice more is

FLUENCY

I read most fluently when

I still need to work on

INDEPENDENT READING

My favorite part of Great Unsolved Mysteries is

A

adequate (A-dih-kwuht) enough

analyze (A-nuh-lyz) to study or examine carefully. An **analysis** (uh-NA-luh-suhs) of something is a careful study of that thing. An **analytical** (a-nuh-LIH-tih-kuhl) person studies something or someone carefully.

architect (AR-kuh-tehkt) a person who plans or designs buildings

assist (uh-SIHST) to take a stand to help

atypical (ay-TIH-pih-kuhl) something not normal or not expected; unusual

C

challenging (CHA-luhn-jihng) taking hard work or skill. A **challenge** (CHA-luhnj) is something that calls for hard work. To **challenge** (CHA-luhnj) means to invite or dare someone to do something difficult.

concept (KAHN-sehpt) an idea. **Conceptual** (kuhn-SEHP-chuh-wuhl) means coming from or belonging to a particular concept or idea. To **conceptualize** (kuhn-SEHP-chuh-wuh-lyz) is to think about an idea and try to picture it.

confining (kahn-FY-nihng) kept within tight limits. To **confine** (kahn-FYN) means to limit or to keep inside. **Confinement** (kahn-FYN-muhnt) is being kept in a tight space.

conquest (KAHN-kwehst) something gained by force or great effort

consist (KAHN-sihst) to be made up of

constant (KAHN-stuhnt) happening all the time or never stopping

constrict (kahn-STRIHKT) to limit movement

construction (kuhn-STRUHK-shuhn) the act or art of making or building something. A **construction** is a building. To **construct** (kahn-STRUHKT) something is to make or build it. **Constructive** (kuhn-STRUHK-tihv) means helpful.

consume (kuhn-SOOM) to eat or use up

continue (kuhn-TIHN-yoo) to keep on happening. **Continuation** (kuhn-tihn-yoo-AY-shuhn) is the process of continuing something without interruption.

contrast (KAHN-trast) a difference. To **contrast** (kuhn-TRAST) two things is to show how they are different.

credit (KREH-diht) praise for something done or achieved; approval or recognition for an accomplishment

D

debate (dih-BAYT) to argue for or against something. A **debate** is a discussion in which people argue for or against something.

defeat (dih-FEET) to beat an enemy or opponent. A **defeat** is a loss.

descendant (dih-SEHN-duhnt) a person who is born to a particular ancestor. To **descend** (dih-SEHND) is to move down.

despite (dih-SPYT) in spite of; regardless of

destructive (dih-STRUHK-tihv) harming people or property. **Destructiveness** (dih-STRUHK-tihv-nuhs) is the power to damage or hurt. To **destroy** (dih-STRAWY) is to ruin something.

dissolve (dih-ZAWLV) to loosen up and become part of a liquid

E

enjoy (ihn-JAWY) to like something. **Enjoyment** (ihn-JAWY-muhnt) means pleasure.

error (ER-uhr) a mistake

essential (ih-SEHN-shuhl) necessary, basic. **Essentially** (ih-SEHNCH-lee) means basically.

expert (EHK-spuhrt) having a lot of skill or knowledge about something. An **expert** is someone who has special knowledge or skill. If you do something **expertly** (EHK-spuhrt-lee), you do it with special skill or knowledge.

export (ehk-SPAWRT) to carry goods out of one country to another

extend (ihk-STEHND) to become longer; to spread or stretch out in length or time

F

feature (FEE-chuhr) an important part of something. To **feature** is to give importance to something; to include or highlight.

focus (FOH-kuhs) to concentrate on something. A **focus** is the center of attention.

foundation (fown-DAY-shuhn) the underlying base or support of a structure; the basis or principle upon which something stands. **Foundational** (fown-DAY-shuh-nuhl) means basic.

fragment (FRAG-muhnt) a piece of something. **Fragmentation** (frag-muhn-TAY-shuhn) is the process of breaking something up into small pieces.

H

historic (hih-STAWR-ihk) something important or worthy of notice because of its relationship to a past event; something remembered for its importance in the past

I

ideal (eye-DEUHL) a worthy idea or goal; a value or idea someone believes in; a high principle

identical (eye-DEHN-tih-kuhl) exactly the same. **Identification** (eye-dehn-tuh-fuh-KAY-shuhn) is a type of document that tells who you are. Your **identity** (eye-DEHN-tuh-tee) is who you are.

image (IH-mihj) a picture or likeness of something. To **imagine** (ih-MA-juhn) is to get an image in your mind. **Imagination** (ih-ma-juh-NAY-shuhn) is the ability to form images and ideas of things never seen or experienced. **Imagery** (IH-mihj-ree) refers to mental pictures.

immense (ih-MEHNTS) something that is very large or great. **Immensely** (ih-MEHNTS-lee) means extremely or very.

immovable (ih-MOO-vuh-buhl) impossible to move or relocate. **Movable** (MOO-vuh-buhl) means easily moved or relocated.

impact (IHM-pakt) the striking of one thing against another or the effect that something has on a person or a thing. To have an **impact** is to have an effect on.

impart (ihm-PAHRT) to pass on knowledge of something

impressive (ihm-PREH-sihv) something noticed right away, usually in a positive way. To **impress** (ihm-PREHS) someone is to make the person notice you for doing something positive. If you are **impressionable** (ihm-PREH-shuhnuh-buhl), you are easily affected by the things you see and hear.

inadequate (ihn-A-dih-kwuht) not enough

incident (IHN-suh-duhnt) something that happens

inclined (ihn-KLYND) leaned a certain way. To **incline** (ihn-KLYN) means to lean toward something. An **inclination** (ihn-kluh-NAY-shuhn) is the way a person is likely to think or behave.

increase (ihn-KREES) to become greater or larger in number or amount

influence (IHN-floo-uhnts) to affect someone or the way something happens

inform (ihn-FAWRM) to give facts or information to someone. **Information** (ihn-fuhr-MAY-shuhn) is facts or details that tell you something. Something that is **informative** (ihn-FAWR-muh-tihv) contains facts.

insert (ihn-SUHRT) to put something into something else

internalize (ihn-TUHR-nuh-lyz) to incorporate ideas, to make them one's own. **Internal** (ihn-TUHR-nuhl) means inside; also, inside the body or within an organization.

involved (ihn-VAWLVD) had a part of or a role in something. To **involve** (ihn-VAWLV) is to include or require something. **Involvement** (ihn-VAWLV-muhnt) means connection to or participation in something.

L

leadership (LEE-duhr-shihp) the ability to lead or give guidance and direction

lessen (LEH-sehn) to shrink in degree or number; to decrease

location (loh-KAY-shuhn) a place. To **locate** (loh-KAYT) means to look for and find something. **Locatable** (lo-KAY-tuh-buhl) means able to be found.

luxuries (LUHK-shuh-reez) items that provide great comfort and that are not affordable for most people

M

maintain (mayn-TAYN) to keep something the way it already is

majestic (muh-JEHS-tihk) very impressive or grand

massive (MA-sihv) huge; often covering a large area. **Massiveness** (MA-sihv-nehs) means hugeness.

meaningful (MEE-nihng-fuhl) important; significant, having a purpose

mental (MEHN-tuhl) having to do with the mind, such as thinking and problem-solving. **Mentally** (MEHN-tuhl-ee) means by using the mind.

merely (MIHR-lee) little and not important. **Mere** (MIHR) means only.

method (MEH-thuhd) a way of or plan for doing something

military (MIH-luh-ter-ee) armed forces; a group of soldiers

modify (MAH-duh-fye) to change something or make it less extreme

N

normal (NAWR-muhl) regular, average, or usual; ordinary

O

occupant (AH-kyuh-puhnt) a person who lives in a building. **Occupy** (AH-kyuh-py) to take up or fill a space; also, to live in a place.

occur (uh-KUHR) to happen; to take place

outcome (AOOT-kuhm) how something turns out

P

partially (PAHR-shuh-lee) means partly or not completely

passage (PA-sihj) a hallway or path through an enclosed area

physical (FIH-zih-kuhl) having to do with the body, not the mind. **Physically** (FIH-sih-kuh-lee) means by using the body's strength.

plunder (PLUHN-duhr) to rob and destroy

portable (PAWR-tuh-buhl) capable of being moved or carried

positive (PAH-suh-tihv) sure or certain of

possess (puh-ZEHS) to have something or to own it. A **possession** (puh-ZEH-shuhn) is an object that belongs to a person. To be **possessive** (puh-ZEH-sihv) means to guard a possession closely.

predict (prih-DIHKT) to say what one thinks will happen in the future. **Prediction** (prih-DIHK-shuhn) refers to a statement of what you think will happen in the future. **Predictable** (prih-DIHK-tuh-buhl) refers to something that can be predicted.

preserve (prih-ZUHRV) to save or keep something safe and free from damage

previous (PREE-vee-uhs) former or coming before

proceed (proh-SEED) to move forward or continue, sometimes after a short pause

profession (pruh-FEH-shuhn) a job or career that requires special training and education

profit (PRAH-fuht) to gain wealth or something of value. A **profit** is wealth gained from something.

progressive (pruh-GREH-sihv) making use of new ideas or moving forward

prominent (PRAH-muh-nuhnt) standing out because of being important or famous

protect (pruh-TEHKT) to guard against. **Protective** (pruh-TEHK-tihv) means wanting to keep something or someone safe.

Q

quantity (KWAHN-tuh-tee) how many or how much of something; an amount or number

R

range (RAYNJ) to be within certain limits

react (ree-AKT) to respond to something. A **reaction** (ree-AK-shuhn) is a response to something.

realm (REHLM) a particular area or a special area of interest; often a kingdom.

recover (ree-KUH-vuhr) to return to a normal or an original state or to get something back

refer (rih-FUHR) to name or talk about

reluctant (rih-LUHK-tuhnt) not willing to do something; opposite of eager

remove (rih-MOOV) to take something away or get rid of it

required (rih-KWIUHRD) must be done

resemble (rih-ZEHM-buhl) to look like something or someone else

resist (rih-ZIHST) to stand up against something

resolve (rih-ZAHLV) to find an answer to a problem or decide to do something

restrict (rih-STRIHKT) to keep something within limits; to limit

revolve (rih-VAHLV) to move in a circle or in circles; to spin

route (ROOT) the way one takes to get somewhere

S

series (SIHR-eez) a group of related things that follow in order. The World **Series** in baseball is a group of seven games that determine which team is the baseball champion.

solve (SAHLV) to release the answer locked in a problem

strict (STRIHKT) keeping tight control over others

T

tempted (TEHMP-tehd) persuaded to do something, often against one's better judgment. To **tempt** (TEHMPT) is to try to convince someone to do something. **Temptation** (TEHMP-tay-shuhn) is a craving or desire for something, especially something forbidden.

tomb (TOOM) a burial place for a dead person

tradition (truh-DIH-shuhn) a custom, an idea, or a belief that is handed down

transport (trants-PAWRT) to carry from one place to another

typical (TIH-pih-kuhl) usual or normal. **Typically** (TIH-pih-kuh-lee) means usually or normally.

U

undertaking (UHN-duhr-TAY-kihng) a project, usually a large one

utilize (YOO-tuh-lyz) to make use of. **Utilization** (yoo-tuh-luh-ZAY-shuhn) is making use of something.